low-carb *magic*

eat good food and lose weight

Publications International, Ltd.

Favorite Brand Name Recipes at www.fbnr.com

Pictured on the front cover: London Broil with Marinated Vegetables *(page 26)*.

Pictured on the back cover *(top to bottom):* Grilled Beef Salad *(page 148)* and Lemon Pepper Chicken *(page 74)*.

ISBN: 1-4127-0256-9

Library of Congress Control Number: 2003110597

Manufactured in China.

8 7 6 5 4 3 2 1

Nutritional Analysis: The nutritional information that appears with each recipe was submitted in part by the participating companies and associations. Every effort has been made to check the accuracy of these numbers. However, because numerous variables account for a wide range of values for certain foods, nutritive analyses in this book should be considered approximate.

Microwave Cooking: Microwave ovens vary in wattage. Use the cooking times as guidelines and check for doneness before adding more time.

Preparation/Cooking Times: Preparation times are based on the approximate amount of time required to assemble the recipe before cooking, baking, chilling or serving. These times include preparation steps such as measuring, chopping and mixing. The fact that some preparations and cooking can be done simultaneously is taken into account. Preparation of optional ingredients and serving suggestions is not included.

Note: Neither Publications International, Ltd., nor the authors, editors or publisher take responsibility for any possible consequences from any treatment, procedure, exercise, dietary modification, action, or applications of medication or preparation by any person reading or following the information in this cookbook. The publication of this book does not constitute the practice of medicine, and this cookbook does not attempt to replace your physician or your pharmacist. **Before undertaking any course of treatment, the authors, editors and publisher advise the reader to check with a physician or other health care provider.**

Contents

Bountiful Beef

Pepper Steak

Prep and Cook Time: 17 minutes

    1 tablespoon coarsely cracked black pepper
   ½ teaspoon dried rosemary
    2 beef filet mignons or rib-eye steaks, 1 inch thick (4 to 6 ounces each)
    1 tablespoon butter or margarine
    1 tablespoon vegetable oil
   ¼ cup brandy or dry red wine

1. Combine pepper and rosemary in bowl. Coat both sides of steaks with mixture.

2. Heat butter and oil in large skillet until hot; add steaks and cook over medium to medium-high heat 5 to 7 minutes per side for medium, or to desired degree of doneness. Remove steaks from skillet. Sprinkle lightly with salt and cover to keep warm.

3. Add brandy to skillet; bring to a boil over high heat, scraping particles from bottom of skillet. Boil about 1 minute or until liquid is reduced by half. Spoon sauce over steaks.

Makes 2 servings

Note: For a special touch, sprinkle chopped parsley over steaks before serving.

NUTRIENTS PER SERVING: Carbohydrate: 2 g, Calories: 392, Fat: 24 g, Protein: 25 g

Beef Pot Roast

2½ pounds beef eye of round roast
1 can (14 ounces) fat-free reduced-sodium beef broth
2 cloves garlic
1 teaspoon herbs de Provence *or* ¼ teaspoon *each* rosemary, thyme, sage and savory
4 small turnips, peeled and cut into wedges
10 ounces fresh brussels sprouts, trimmed
8 ounces baby carrots
4 ounces pearl onions, skins removed
1 tablespoon water
2 teaspoons cornstarch

1. Heat large nonstick skillet over medium-high heat. Place roast, fat side down, in skillet. Cook until evenly browned. Remove roast from skillet; place in Dutch oven.

2. Pour broth into Dutch oven; bring to a boil over high heat. Add garlic and herbs de Provence. Cover and reduce heat; simmer 1½ hours.

3. Add turnips, brussels sprouts, carrots and onions to Dutch oven. Cover; cook 25 to 30 minutes or until vegetables are tender. Remove meat and vegetables and arrange on serving platter; cover with foil to keep warm.

4. Strain broth; return to Dutch oven. Stir water into cornstarch until smooth. Stir cornstarch mixture into broth. Bring to a boil over medium-high heat; cook and stir 1 minute or until thick and bubbly. Serve immediately with pot roast and vegetables. Garnish as desired.   *Makes 8 servings*

NUTRIENTS PER SERVING: Carbohydrate: 11 g, Calories: 261, Fat: 9 g, Protein: 35 g

Beef Pot Roast

Jamaican Steak

2 pounds beef flank steak
¼ cup packed brown sugar
3 tablespoons orange juice
3 tablespoons lime juice
3 cloves garlic, minced
1 piece (1½×1 inches) fresh ginger, minced
2 teaspoons grated orange peel
2 teaspoons grated lime peel
1 teaspoon salt
1 teaspoon black pepper
¼ teaspoon ground cinnamon
⅛ teaspoon ground cloves
   Shredded orange peel
   Shredded lime peel

Score both sides of beef.* Combine sugar, juices, garlic, ginger, grated peels, salt, pepper, cinnamon and cloves in 2-quart glass dish. Add beef; turn to coat. Cover and refrigerate steak at least 2 hours. Remove beef from marinade; discard marinade. Grill beef over medium-hot KINGSFORD® Briquets about 6 minutes per side until medium-rare or to desired doneness. Garnish with shredded orange and lime peels.   *Makes 6 servings*

*To score flank steak, cut ¼-inch-deep diagonal lines about 1 inch apart in surface of steak to form diamond-shaped design.

NUTRIENTS PER SERVING: Carbohydrate: 0 g, Calories: 283, Fat: 17 g, Protein: 30 g

Stir-Fry Beef & Vegetable Soup

Prep and Cook Time: 22 minutes

1 pound boneless beef steak, such as sirloin or round steak
2 teaspoons dark sesame oil, divided
3 cans (about 14 ounces each) reduced-sodium beef broth
1 package (16 ounces) frozen stir-fry vegetables
3 green onions, thinly sliced
¼ cup stir-fry sauce

1. Slice beef across grain into ⅛-inch-thick strips; cut strips into bite-size pieces.

2. Heat Dutch oven over high heat. Add 1 teaspoon sesame oil and tilt pan to coat bottom. Add half the beef in single layer; cook 1 minute, without stirring, until slightly browned on bottom. Turn and brown other side about 1 minute. Remove beef from pan; set aside. Repeat with remaining 1 teaspoon sesame oil and beef; set aside.

3. Add broth to Dutch oven; cover and bring to a boil over high heat. Add vegetables; reduce heat to medium-high and simmer 3 to 5 minutes or until heated through. Add beef, green onions and stir-fry sauce; simmer 1 minute.   *Makes 6 servings*

NUTRIENTS PER SERVING: Carbohydrate: 7 g, Calories: 159, Fat: 5 g, Protein: 20 g

Stir-Fry Beef & Vegetable Soup

Grilled Italian Steak

¾ cup WISH-BONE® Italian Dressing*
2 tablespoons grated Parmesan cheese
2 teaspoons dried basil leaves, crushed
¼ teaspoon cracked black pepper
2 to 3-pound boneless sirloin or top round steak

Also terrific with WISH-BONE® Robusto Italian or Lite Italian Dressing.

In large, shallow nonaluminum baking dish or plastic bag, combine all ingredients except steak. Add steak; turn to coat. Cover or close bag and marinate in refrigerator, turning occasionally, 3 to 24 hours.

Remove steak from marinade, reserving marinade. Grill or broil steak, turning once, until steak is done.

Meanwhile, in small saucepan, bring reserved marinade to a boil and continue boiling 1 minute. Pour over steak. *Makes 8 servings*

NUTRIENTS PER SERVING: Carbohydrate: 3 g, Calories: 310, Fat: 19 g, Protein: 32 g

Hamburger Casserole Olé

Prep Time: 15 minutes   *Cook Time:* 25 to 30 minutes

1 pound lean ground beef or ground turkey
1 package (1¼ ounces) taco seasoning mix
1 cup water
1 box (9 ounces) BIRDS EYE® frozen Cut Green Beans
½ cup shredded sharp Cheddar cheese
½ cup shredded mozzarella cheese

• Preheat oven to 325°F.

• Brown beef; drain excess fat. Add taco mix and water; cook over low heat 8 to 10 minutes or until liquid has been absorbed.

• Meanwhile, cook green beans according to package directions; drain.

• Spread meat in greased 13×9 inch baking pan. Spread beans over meat. Sprinkle with cheeses.

• Bake 15 to 20 minutes or until hot and cheese is melted.   *Makes 4 servings*

Tip: Try substituting plain low-fat yogurt for sour cream in your recipes for a lighter version.

NUTRIENTS PER SERVING: Carbohydrate: 9 g, Calories: 467, Fat: 30 g, Protein: 36 g

Rosemary Steak

4 boneless top loin beef steaks or New York strip steaks (about 6 ounces each)
2 tablespoons minced fresh rosemary
2 cloves garlic, minced
1 tablespoon extra-virgin olive oil
1 teaspoon grated lemon peel
1 teaspoon coarsely ground black pepper
½ teaspoon salt
   Fresh rosemary sprigs

Score steaks in diamond pattern on both sides. Combine minced rosemary, garlic, oil, lemon peel, pepper and salt in small bowl; rub mixture onto surface of meat. Cover and refrigerate at least 15 minutes. Grill steaks over medium-hot KINGSFORD® Briquets about 4 minutes per side until medium-rare or to desired doneness. Cut steaks diagonally into ½-inch-thick slices. Garnish with rosemary sprigs. *Makes 4 servings*

NUTRIENTS PER SERVING: Carbohydrate: 1 g, Calories: 328, Fat: 16 g, Protein: 42 g

Italian-Style Meat Loaf

  1 can (6 ounces) no-salt-added tomato paste
½ cup dry red wine plus ½ cup water *or* 1 cup water
  1 teaspoon minced garlic
½ teaspoon dried basil leaves
½ teaspoon dried oregano leaves
¼ teaspoon salt
12 ounces lean ground round
12 ounces ground turkey breast
  1 cup fresh whole wheat bread crumbs (2 slices whole wheat bread)
½ cup shredded zucchini
¼ cup cholesterol-free egg substitute *or* 2 egg whites

1. Preheat oven to 350°F. Combine tomato paste, wine, water, garlic, basil, oregano and salt in small saucepan. Bring to a boil; reduce heat to low. Simmer, uncovered, 15 minutes. Set aside.

2. Combine beef, turkey, bread crumbs, zucchini, egg substitute and ½ cup reserved tomato mixture in large bowl. Mix well. Shape into loaf; place into ungreased 9×5×3-inch loaf pan. Bake 45 minutes. Discard any drippings. Pour ½ cup remaining tomato mixture over top of loaf. Bake an additional 15 minutes. Place on serving platter. Cool 10 minutes before slicing. Garnish as desired.   *Makes 8 servings*

NUTRIENTS PER SERVING: Carbohydrate: 7 g, Calories: 144, Fat: 2 g, Protein: 19 g

Italian-Style Meat Loaf

Veal in Gingered Sweet Bell Pepper Sauce

1 teaspoon olive oil
3/4 pound veal cutlets, thinly sliced
1/2 cup skim milk
1 tablespoon finely chopped fresh tarragon
2 teaspoons crushed capers
1 jar (7 ounces) roasted red peppers, drained
1 tablespoon lemon juice
1/2 teaspoon freshly grated ginger
1/2 teaspoon black pepper

1. Heat oil in medium saucepan over high heat. Add veal; lightly brown both sides. Reduce heat to medium. Add milk, chopped tarragon and capers. Cook, uncovered, 5 minutes or until veal is fork-tender and milk evaporates.

2. Place roasted peppers, lemon juice, ginger and black pepper in food processor or blender; process until smooth. Set aside.

3. Remove veal from pan with slotted spoon; place in serving dish. Spoon roasted pepper sauce over veal. Sprinkle with cooked capers and fresh tarragon, if desired.

Makes 4 servings

NUTRIENTS PER SERVING: Carbohydrate: 6 g, Calories: 120, Fat: 4 g, Protein: 14 g

Veal in Gingered Sweet Bell Pepper Sauce

Simmering Fondue

Prep and Cook Time: 20 minutes

1 pound medium shrimp, peeled
8 ounces beef tenderloin, cut into thin slices
8 ounces lamb loin, cut into thin slices
2 cups sliced mushrooms
2 cups sliced carrots
2 cups broccoli florets
4 cans (about 14 ounces each) reduced-sodium chicken broth
½ cup dry white wine
1 tablespoon chopped fresh parsley
1 teaspoon minced garlic
½ teaspoon dried thyme leaves
½ teaspoon dried rosemary

1. Arrange shrimp, beef, lamb, mushrooms, carrots and broccoli on large serving platter or in individual bowls.

2. Combine chicken broth, wine, parsley, garlic, thyme and rosemary in large saucepan. Bring to a boil over high heat. Remove from heat. Strain broth. Transfer broth to electric wok. Return to a simmer over high heat.

3. Thread any combination shrimp, meat and vegetables onto bamboo skewer or fondue fork. Cook in broth 2 to 3 minutes.   *Makes 4 servings*

NUTRIENTS PER SERVING: Carbohydrate: 10 g, Calories: 334, Fat: 10 g, Protein: 50 g

Joe's Special

Prep and Cook Time: 20 minutes

> 1 pound lean ground beef
> 2 cups sliced mushrooms
> 1 small onion, chopped
> 2 teaspoons Worcestershire sauce
> 1 teaspoon dried oregano leaves
> 1 teaspoon ground nutmeg
> ½ teaspoon garlic powder
> ½ teaspoon salt
> 1 package (10 ounces) frozen chopped spinach, thawed
> 4 large eggs, lightly beaten
> ⅓ cup grated Parmesan cheese

1. Spray large skillet with nonstick cooking spray. Add ground beef, mushrooms and onion; cook over medium-high heat 6 to 8 minutes or until onion is tender, breaking beef apart with wooden spoon. Add Worcestershire, oregano, nutmeg, garlic powder and salt. Cook until meat is no longer pink.

2. Drain spinach (do not squeeze dry); stir into meat mixture. Push mixture to one side of pan. Reduce heat to medium. Pour eggs into other side of pan; cook, without stirring, 1 to 2 minutes or until set on bottom. Lift eggs to allow uncooked portion to flow underneath. Repeat until softly set. Gently stir into meat mixture and heat through. Stir in cheese.

Makes 4 to 6 servings

NUTRIENTS PER SERVING: Carbohydrate: 8 g, Calories: 369, Fat: 23 g, Protein: 32 g

Salisbury Steaks with Mushroom-Wine Sauce

Prep and Cook Time: 20 minutes

1 pound lean ground beef sirloin
¾ teaspoon garlic salt or seasoned salt
¼ teaspoon black pepper
2 tablespoons butter or margarine
1 package (8 ounces) sliced button mushrooms *or* 2 packages (4 ounces each) sliced exotic mushrooms
2 tablespoons sweet vermouth or ruby port wine
1 jar (12 ounces) *or* 1 can (10½ ounces) beef gravy

1. Heat large heavy nonstick skillet over medium-high heat 3 minutes or until hot.* Meanwhile, combine ground sirloin, garlic salt and pepper; mix well. Shape mixture into four ¼-inch-thick oval patties.

2. Place patties in skillet as they are formed; cook 3 minutes per side or until browned. Transfer to plate. Pour off drippings.

3. Melt butter in skillet; add mushrooms. Cook and stir 2 minutes. Add vermouth; cook 1 minute. Add gravy; mix well.

4. Return patties to skillet; simmer uncovered over medium heat 2 minutes for medium or until desired doneness, turning meat and stirring sauce.   *Makes 4 servings*

*If pan is not heavy, use medium heat.

Note: For a special touch, sprinkle steaks with chopped parsley or chives.

NUTRIENTS PER SERVING: Carbohydrate: 8 g, Calories: 341, Fat: 23 g, Protein: 24 g

Beef with Dry Spice Rub

3 tablespoons firmly packed brown sugar
1 tablespoon black peppercorns
1 tablespoon yellow mustard seeds
1 tablespoon whole coriander seeds
4 cloves garlic
1½ to 2 pounds beef top round steak or London Broil, about ½ inch thick
    Vegetable or olive oil
    Salt

Place sugar, peppercorns, mustard seeds, coriander seeds and garlic in blender or food processor; process until seeds and garlic are crushed. Rub beef with oil; pat on spice mixture. Season generously with salt.

Lightly oil hot grid to prevent sticking. Grill beef on covered grill over medium-low KINGSFORD® Briquets 16 to 20 minutes for medium or until desired doneness, turning once. Let stand 5 minutes before cutting across the grain into thin diagonal slices.

Makes 6 servings

NUTRIENTS PER SERVING: Carbohydrate: 9 g, Calories: 249, Fat: 11 g, Protein: 29 g

London Broil with Marinated Vegetables

¾ **cup olive oil**
¾ **cup red wine**
2 **tablespoons red wine vinegar**
2 **tablespoons finely chopped shallots**
2 **teaspoons minced garlic**
½ **teaspoon dried marjoram leaves**
½ **teaspoon dried oregano leaves**
½ **teaspoon dried basil leaves**
½ **teaspoon black pepper**
2 **pounds top round London broil (1½ inches thick)**
1 **medium red onion, cut into ¼-inch-thick slices**
1 **package (8 ounces) sliced mushrooms**
1 **medium red bell pepper, cut into strips**
1 **medium zucchini, cut into ¼-inch-thick slices**

Combine olive oil, wine, vinegar, shallots, garlic, marjoram, oregano, basil and pepper in medium bowl; whisk to combine. Combine London broil and ¾ cup marinade in large resealable food storage bag. Seal bag and turn to coat. Marinate up to 24 hours in refrigerator, turning once or twice. Combine vegetables and remaining marinade in separate large food storage bag. Seal bag and turn to coat. Refrigerate up to 24 hours, turning once or twice.

Preheat broiler. Remove meat from marinade and place on broiler pan; discard marinade. Broil 4 to 5 inches from heat about 9 minutes per side or until desired doneness. Let stand 10 minutes before slicing. Cut meat into thin slices. While meat is standing, drain marinade from vegetables and arrange on broiler pan. Broil 4 to 5 inches from heat about 9 minutes or until edges of vegetables just begin to brown. Serve meat and vegetables immediately on platter. *Makes 6 servings*

NUTRIENTS PER SERVING: Carbohydrate: 8 g, Calories: 324, Fat: 16 g, Protein: 36 g

London Broil with Marinated Vegetables

Fragrant Beef with Garlic Sauce

1 boneless beef top sirloin steak, cut 1 inch thick (about 1¼ pounds)
⅓ cup reduced-sodium teriyaki sauce
10 large cloves garlic, peeled
½ cup defatted low-sodium beef broth

1. Place beef in large plastic bag. Pour teriyaki sauce over beef. Close bag securely; turn to coat. Marinate in refrigerator at least 30 minutes or up to 4 hours.

2. Combine garlic and broth in small saucepan. Bring to a boil over high heat. Reduce heat to medium. Simmer, uncovered, 5 minutes. Cover and simmer 8 to 9 minutes until garlic is softened. Transfer to blender or food processor; process until smooth.

3. Meanwhile, drain beef; reserve marinade. Place beef on rack of broiler pan. Brush with half of reserved marinade. Broil 5 to 6 inches from heat 5 minutes. Turn beef over; brush with remaining marinade. Broil 5 minutes more.*

4. Slice beef thinly; serve with garlic sauce.   *Makes 4 servings*

*Broiling time is for medium-rare doneness. Adjust time for desired doneness.

NUTRIENTS PER SERVING: Carbohydrate: 6 g, Calories: 212, Fat: 6 g, Protein: 33 g

Fragrant Beef with Garlic Sauce

Peppered Beef Rib Roast

1½ tablespoons black peppercorns
1 boneless beef rib roast (2½ to 3 pounds), well trimmed
¼ cup Dijon mustard
2 cloves garlic, minced
Sour Cream Sauce (recipe follows)

Prepare grill for indirect cooking.

Place peppercorns in small resealable plastic food storage bag. Squeeze out excess air; close bag securely. Pound peppercorns using flat side of meat mallet or rolling pin until cracked. Set aside.

Pat roast dry with paper towels. Combine mustard and garlic in small bowl; spread over top and sides of roast. Sprinkle pepper over mustard mixture.

Place roast, pepper-side up, on grid directly over drip pan. Grill, covered, over medium heat 1 hour to 1 hour 10 minutes for medium or until internal temperature reaches 145°F when tested with meat thermometer inserted into the thickest part of roast, adding 4 to 9 briquets to both sides of the fire after 45 minutes to maintain medium heat.

Meanwhile, prepare Sour Cream Sauce. Cover; refrigerate until serving.

Transfer roast to cutting board; cover with foil. Let stand 10 to 15 minutes before carving. Internal temperature will continue to rise 5°F to 10°F during stand time. Serve with Sour Cream Sauce. *Makes 6 to 8 servings*

Sour Cream Sauce: Combine ¾ cup sour cream, 2 tablespoons prepared horseradish, 1 tablespoon balsamic vinegar and ½ teaspoon sugar in small bowl; mix well.

NUTRIENTS PER SERVING: Carbohydrate: 5 g, Calories: 441, Fat: 23 g, Protein: 52 g

Peppered Beef Rib Roast

Palate-Pleasing Pork

Pork Tenderloin with Sherry-Mushroom Sauce

  1 pork tenderloin (1 to 1½ pounds)
1½ cups chopped button mushrooms or shiitake mushroom caps
  2 tablespoons sliced green onion
  1 clove garlic, minced
  1 tablespoon reduced-fat margarine
  1 tablespoon cornstarch
  1 tablespoon chopped fresh parsley
  ½ teaspoon dried thyme leaves
    Dash black pepper
  ⅓ cup water
  1 tablespoon dry sherry
  ½ teaspoon beef bouillon granules

Preheat oven to 375°F. Place pork on rack in shallow baking pan. Insert meat thermometer into thickest part of tenderloin. Roast, uncovered, 25 to 35 minutes or until thermometer registers 165°F. Let stand, covered, 5 to 10 minutes while preparing sauce.

Cook and stir mushrooms, green onion and garlic in margarine in small saucepan over medium heat until vegetables are tender. Stir in cornstarch, parsley, thyme and pepper. Stir in water, sherry and bouillon granules. Cook and stir until sauce boils and thickens. Cook and stir 2 minutes more. Slice pork; serve with sauce.   *Makes 4 servings*

NUTRIENTS PER SERVING: Carbohydrate: 4 g, Calories: 179, Fat: 6 g, Protein: 26 g

Blackberry-Glazed Pork Medallions

⅓ cup no-sugar-added seedless blackberry spread
4½ teaspoons red wine vinegar
1 tablespoon sugar
¼ teaspoon red pepper flakes
1 teaspoon vegetable oil
1 pound pork tenderloin, cut in ¼-inch slices
¼ teaspoon dried thyme leaves, divided
¼ teaspoon salt, divided

Whisk blackberry spread, vinegar, sugar and red pepper flakes in small bowl until blended; set aside.

Heat large nonstick skillet over medium-high heat until hot. Coat skillet with nonstick cooking spray; add oil and tilt skillet to coat bottom. Add half of pork slices; sprinkle with half of thyme and half of salt. Cook 2 minutes; turn and cook 1 minute on other side. Remove pork from skillet and set aside. Repeat with remaining pork, thyme and salt.

Add blackberry mixture to skillet; bring to a boil over high heat. Add reserved pork slices, discarding any accumulated juices. Cook about 4 minutes, turning constantly, until pork is richly glazed. *Makes 4 servings*

NUTRIENTS PER SERVING: Carbohydrate: 10 g, Calories: 186, Fat: 5 g, Protein: 23 g

Blackberry-Glazed Pork Medallions

Lemon-Capered Pork Tenderloin

1½ **pounds boneless pork tenderloin**
1 **tablespoon crushed capers**
1 **teaspoon dried rosemary**
⅛ **teaspoon black pepper**
1 **cup water**
¼ **cup lemon juice**

1. Preheat oven to 350°F. Trim fat from tenderloin; discard. Set tenderloin aside.

2. Combine capers, rosemary and black pepper in small bowl. Rub rosemary mixture over tenderloin. Place tenderloin in shallow roasting pan. Pour water and lemon juice over tenderloin.

3. Bake, uncovered, 1 hour or until thermometer inserted in thickest part of tenderloin registers 170°F. Remove from oven; cover with aluminum foil. Allow to stand 10 minutes before serving. Garnish as desired.   *Makes 8 servings*

NUTRIENTS PER SERVING: Carbohydrate: <1 g, Calories: 114, Fat: 3 g, Protein: 19 g

Lemon-Capered Pork Tenderloin

Ham & Cheddar Frittata

3 large eggs
3 large egg whites
½ teaspoon salt
½ teaspoon freshly ground black pepper
1½ cups (4 ounces) frozen broccoli florets, thawed
6 ounces deli smoked ham, cut into ½-inch thick cubes (1¼ cups)
⅓ cup drained bottled roasted red bell peppers, sliced into thin strips
1 tablespoon butter
½ cup (2 ounces) shredded sharp Cheddar cheese

1. Preheat broiler with rack about 5 inches from heat.

2. Beat together eggs, egg whites, salt and pepper in large bowl. Add broccoli, ham and pepper strips; mix well.

3. Melt butter over medium heat in 10-inch ovenproof skillet with sloped sides. Add egg mixture to skillet; cover. Cook 5 to 6 minutes or until eggs are set around edges. (Center will be wet.)

4. Uncover; sprinkle cheese over frittata. Transfer to broiler and broil 2 minutes or until eggs are set in center and cheese is melted. Let stand 5 minutes; cut into wedges.

Makes 4 servings

NUTRIENTS PER SERVING: Carbohydrate: 4 g, Calories: 209, Fat: 13 g, Protein: 19 g

Peppered Pork Cutlets with Onion Gravy

½ teaspoon paprika
¼ teaspoon ground cumin
⅛ teaspoon cayenne pepper (optional)
¼ teaspoon black pepper
4 boneless pork cutlets (4 ounces each), trimmed of fat
2 cups thinly sliced onion
2 tablespoons flour, divided
¾ cup water
1½ teaspoons chicken bouillon granules
2 tablespoons fat-free milk
¼ teaspoon salt

1. In a small bowl, combine paprika, cumin, cayenne, if desired, and pepper; blend well. Sprinkle mixture evenly over one side of each cutlet and press down gently to adhere. If time allows, let stand 15 minutes to absorb flavors.

2. Heat a large nonstick skillet over medium heat. Coat skillet with nonstick cooking spray. Add pork, seasoned side down, and cook 3 minutes or until richly browned. Remove from skillet and set aside on a plate, seasoned side up.

3. Increase heat to medium high, coat skillet with cooking spray, add onions to pan, and cook 4 minutes or until richly browned, stirring frequently. Sprinkle with 1½ tablespoons flour; toss to coat. Add water and bouillon, stir to blend and bring to a boil. Add cooked pork and any accumulated juices; spoon some of the sauce over pork. Reduce heat, cover, and simmer 20 minutes, or until pork is no longer pink in center.

4. Place pork on a serving platter and set aside. Stir milk into onion mixture, or, for thicker consistency, blend together milk and ½ tablespoon flour and add to onion mixture. Add salt and cook 1 to 2 minutes. Spoon sauce over and around pork.   *Makes 4 servings*

NUTRIENTS PER SERVING: Carbohydrate: 7 g, Calories: 200, Fat: 6 g, Protein: 26 g

Honey-Glazed Pork

1 large or 2 small pork tenderloins (about 1¼ pounds)
¼ cup soy sauce
2 cloves garlic, minced
3 tablespoons honey
2 tablespoons brown sugar
1 teaspoon minced fresh ginger
1 tablespoon toasted sesame seeds*

*To toast sesame seeds, spread seeds in small skillet. Shake skillet over medium heat 2 minutes or until seeds begin to pop and turn golden.

1. Place pork in large resealable plastic bag. Combine soy sauce and garlic in small cup; pour over pork. Seal bag; turn to coat. Marinate in refrigerator up to 2 hours.

2. Preheat oven to 400°F. Drain pork; reserve 1 tablespoon marinade. Combine honey, brown sugar, ginger and reserved marinade in small bowl.

3. Place pork in shallow, foil-lined roasting pan. Brush with half of honey mixture. Roast 10 minutes. Turn pork over; brush with remaining honey mixture and sprinkle with sesame seeds. Roast 10 minutes for small or 15 minutes for large tenderloin or until internal temperature reaches 165°F when tested with meat thermometer inserted into the thickest part of roast.

4. Transfer roast to cutting board; cover with foil. Let stand 10 to 15 minutes. Internal temperature will continue to rise 5°F to 10°F during stand time. Cut pork across the grain into ½-inch slices. Serve with pan juices, if desired.   *Makes 4 servings*

NUTRIENTS PER SERVING: Carbohydrate: 8 g, Calories: 203, Fat: 5 g, Protein: 31 g

Mustard-Crusted Roast Pork

3 tablespoons Dijon mustard
4 teaspoons minced garlic, divided
2 whole well-trimmed pork tenderloins (about 1 pound each)
2 tablespoons dried thyme leaves
1 teaspoon black pepper
½ teaspoon salt
1 pound asparagus spears, ends trimmed
2 red or yellow bell peppers (or one of each), cut lengthwise into ½-inch-wide strips
1 cup fat-free reduced-sodium chicken broth, divided

1. Preheat oven to 375°F. Combine mustard and 3 teaspoons garlic in small bowl. Place tenderloins on waxed paper; spread mustard mixture evenly over top and sides of both tenderloins. Combine thyme, black pepper and salt in small bowl; reserve 1 teaspoon mixture. Sprinkle remaining mixture evenly over tenderloins, patting so that seasoning adheres to mustard. Place tenderloins on rack in shallow roasting pan. Roast 25 minutes.

2. Arrange asparagus and bell peppers in single layer in shallow casserole or 13×9-inch baking pan. Add ¼ cup broth, reserved thyme mixture and remaining 1 teaspoon garlic; toss to coat.

3. Roast vegetables in oven, alongside pork tenderloins,15 to 20 minutes or until thermometer inserted into center of pork registers 160°F and vegetables are tender. Transfer tenderloins to carving board; tent with foil and let stand 5 minutes. Arrange vegetables on serving platter, reserving juices in dish; cover and keep warm. Add remaining ¾ cup broth and juices in dish to roasting pan. Place over range-top burner(s); simmer 3 to 4 minutes over medium-high heat or until juices are reduced to ¾ cup, stirring frequently. Carve tenderloin crosswise into ¼-inch slices; arrange on serving platter. Spoon juices over tenderloin and vegetables.
Makes 8 servings

NUTRIENTS PER SERVING: Carbohydrate: 8 g, Calories: 182, Fat: 5 g, Protein: 27 g

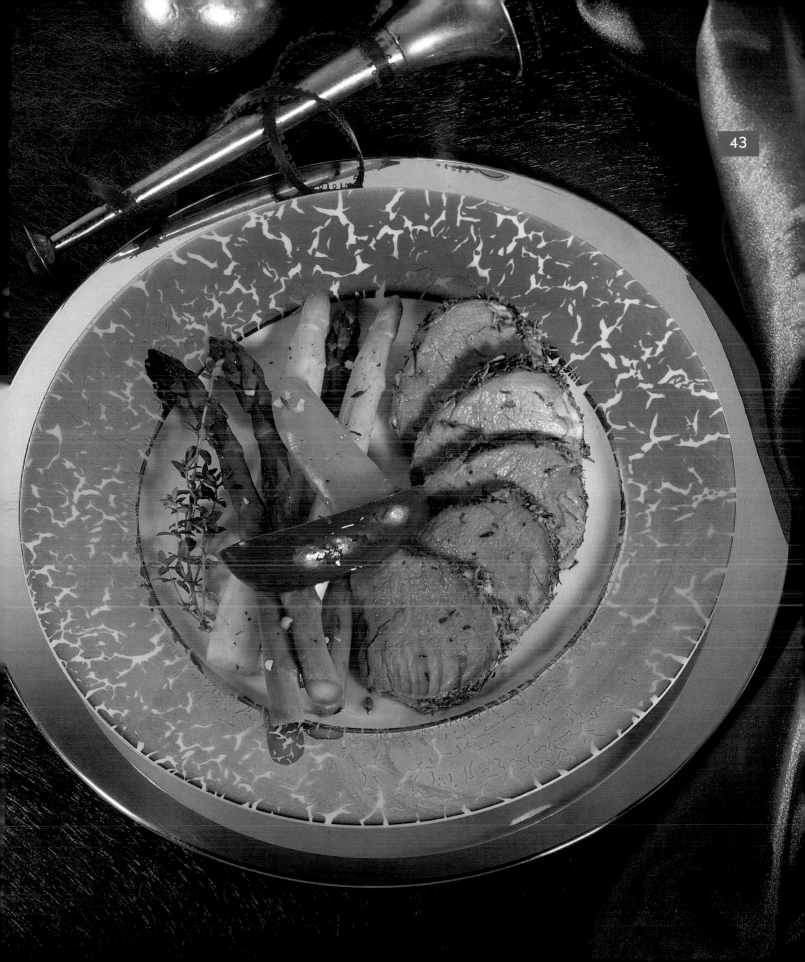

Pork Chops Paprikash

2 teaspoons butter

1 medium onion, very thinly sliced

1¼ teaspoons paprika, divided

1 teaspoon garlic salt

½ teaspoon freshly ground black pepper

4 (5- to 6-ounce) bone-in center cut pork chops, well trimmed (about ½ inch thick)

⅓ cup well-drained sauerkraut

⅓ cup light or regular sour cream

1. Preheat broiler with rack 4 to 5 inches from heat.

2. Melt butter in large skillet over medum-high heat. Separate onion slices into rings; add to skillet. Cook, stirring occasionally, until golden brown and tender, about 10 minutes.

3. Meanwhile, sprinkle 1 teaspoon paprika, garlic salt and pepper over both sides of pork chops. Place chops on rack of broiler pan.

4. Broil 5 minutes. Turn and broil until chops are no longer pink in center, 4 to 5 minutes.

5. Combine cooked onion with sauerkraut, sour cream and remaining ¼ teaspoon paprika; mix well. Granish chops with onion mixture, or spread onion mixture over chops and return to broiler. Broil just until hot, about 1 minute.   *Makes 4 servings*

NUTRIENTS PER SERVING: Carbohydrate: 5 g, Calories: 226, Fat: 14 g, Protein: 19 g

Pork Chop Paprikash

Peanut Pork Tenderloin

⅓ **cup chunky unsweetened peanut butter**
⅓ **cup regular or light canned coconut milk**
¼ **cup lemon juice or dry white wine**
3 **tablespoons soy sauce**
3 **cloves garlic, minced**
2 **tablespoons sugar**
1 **piece (1-inch cube) fresh ginger, minced**
½ **teaspoon salt**
¼ **to** ½ **teaspoon cayenne pepper**
¼ **teaspoon ground cinnamon**
1½ **pounds pork tenderloin**

Combine peanut butter, coconut milk, lemon juice, soy sauce, garlic, sugar, ginger, salt, cayenne pepper and cinnamon in 2-quart glass dish until blended. Add pork; turn to coat. Cover and refrigerate at least 30 minutes or overnight. Remove pork from marinade; discard marinade. Grill pork on covered grill over medium KINGSFORD® Briquets about 20 minutes until just barely pink in center, turning 4 times. Cut crosswise into ½-inch slices. Serve immediately. *Makes 4 to 6 servings*

NUTRIENTS PER SERVING: Carbohydrate: 2 g, Calories: 248, Fat: 8 g, Protein: 39 g

Roasted Pork

3 tablespoons barbecue sauce
1 tablespoon low-sodium soy sauce
1 tablespoon dry sherry
2 cloves garlic, minced
½ teaspoon crushed Szechuan peppercorns or red pepper flakes
2 whole pork tenderloins (about 1¼ to 1½ pounds total)

1. Preheat oven to 350°F. Combine barbecue sauce, soy sauce, sherry, garlic and peppercorns in small bowl.

2. Brush one-fourth of mixture evenly over each roast. Place roasts on rack in shallow foil-lined roasting pan. Cook roasts 15 minutes; turn and brush with remaining barbecue sauce mixture. Continue to cook until internal temperature reaches 165°F when tested with meat thermometer inserted in thickest part of roast. (Timing will depend on thickness of pork; test at 30 minutes.)

3. Transfer roast to cutting board; cover with foil. Let stand 10 to 15 minutes before carving. Internal temperature will continue to rise 5°F to 10°F during stand time. Slice diagonally and serve warm with rice, if desired. Or, for use in other recipes, cut into portions and refrigerate up to 3 days or freeze up to 3 months.   *Makes 4 servings*

Variation: For Chinese Barbecued Pork, add 1 teaspoon red food coloring to barbecue sauce mixture. Prepare roasts as recipe directs. Roasts may be grilled over medium coals until an internal temperature of 155°F is reached. (Turn pork after 8 minutes; check temperature at 16 minutes.)

NUTRIENTS PER SERVING: Carbohydrate: 3 g, Calories: 199, Fat: 5 g, Protein: 32 g

Pork Medallions with Marsala

Prep & Cook Time: 20 minutes

1 pound pork tenderloin, cut into ½-inch slices
All-purpose flour
2 tablespoons olive oil
1 clove garlic, minced
½ cup sweet Marsala wine
2 tablespoons chopped fresh parsley

1. Lightly dust pork with flour. Heat oil in large skillet over medium-high heat until hot. Add pork slices; cook 3 minutes per side or until browned. Remove from pan. Reduce heat to medium.

2. Add garlic to skillet; cook and stir 1 minute. Add wine and pork; cook 3 minutes or until pork is barely pink in center. Remove pork from skillet. Stir in parsley. Simmer wine mixture until slightly thickened, 2 to 3 minutes. Serve over pork.   *Makes 4 servings*

Tip: For a special touch, sprinkle with chopped red onion just before serving.

Note: Marsala is rich smoky-flavored wine imported from the Mediterranean island of Sicily. This sweet varietal is served with dessert or used for cooking. Dry Marsala is served as a before-dinner drink.

NUTRIENTS PER SERVING: Carbohydrate: 1 g, Calories: 218, Fat: 11 g, Protein: 24 g

Spinach & Egg Casserole

Prep Time: 10 minutes   *Cook Time:* 15 to 20 minutes

1 box (10 ounces) BIRDS EYE® frozen Chopped Spinach
1 can (15 ounces) Cheddar cheese soup
1 tablespoon mustard
½ pound deli ham, cut into ¼-inch cubes
4 hard-boiled eggs, chopped or sliced

- Preheat oven to 350°F.

- In large saucepan, cook spinach according to package directions; drain well.

- Stir in soup, mustard and ham.

- Pour into 9×9-inch baking pan. Top with eggs.

- Bake 15 to 20 minutes or until heated through.   *Makes 4 servings*

Serving Suggestion: Sprinkle with paprika for added color.

Tip: Cook eggs the day before and refrigerate. They will be much easier to peel.

NUTRIENTS PER SERVING: Carbohydrate: 4 g, Calories: 234, Fat: 14 g, Protein: 21 g

Spinach & Egg Casserole

Spicy Caribbean Pork Medallions

6 ounces pork tenderloin
1 teaspoon Caribbean jerk seasoning
   Nonstick olive oil cooking spray
1/3 cup pineapple juice
1 teaspoon brown mustard
1/2 teaspoon cornstarch

1. Cut tenderloin into 1/2-inch-thick slices. Place each slice between 2 pieces of plastic wrap. Pound to 1/4-inch thickness. Rub both sides of pork pieces with jerk seasoning.

2. Lightly spray large nonstick skillet with cooking spray; heat over medium heat until hot. Add pork. Cook 2 to 3 minutes or until no longer pink, turning once. Remove from skillet. Keep warm.

3. Stir together pineapple juice, mustard and cornstarch until smooth. Add to skillet. Cook and stir over medium heat until mixture comes to a boil and thickens slightly. Spoon over pork. *Makes 2 servings*

NUTRIENTS PER SERVING: Carbohydrate: 7 g, Calories: 134, Fat: 3 g, Protein: 18 g

Zesty Skillet Pork Chops

    1 teaspoon chili powder
    ½ teaspoon salt, divided
 1¼ pounds lean pork chops, well trimmed of fat
    2 cups diced tomatoes
    1 cup chopped green, red or yellow bell pepper
    ¾ cup thinly sliced celery
    ½ cup chopped onion
    1 teaspoon dried thyme leaves
    1 tablespoon hot pepper sauce
       Nonstick cooking spray
    2 tablespoons finely chopped parsley

1. Rub chili powder and ¼ teaspoon salt evenly over one side of pork chops.

2. Combine tomatoes, bell pepper, celery, onion, thyme and pepper sauce in medium mixing bowl; stir to blend.

3. Lightly coat 12-inch nonstick skillet with cooking spray. Heat over medium-high heat until hot. Add pork chops, seasoned side down; cook 1 minute. Turn pork; top with tomato mixture.

4. Bring to boil. Reduce heat and simmer, covered, 25 minutes or until pork is tender and mixture has thickened.

5. Transfer pork to serving plates. Increase heat; bring tomato mixture to a boil and cook 2 minutes or until most of the liquid has evaporated. Remove from heat; stir in parsley and remaining ¼ teaspoon salt and spoon over pork. *Makes 4 servings*

NUTRIENTS PER SERVING: Carbohydrate: 9 g, Calories: 172, Fat: 7 g, Protein: 20 g

Pork Tenderloin Paprikash

1 pork tenderloin (1 pound) well-trimmed
2 teaspoons paprika
¼ teaspoon salt
⅛ teaspoon ground red pepper or hot paprika
⅓ cup well-drained bottled sauerkraut
⅓ cup nonfat or reduced-fat sour cream
   Chopped fresh dill and dill sprigs (optional)

1. Preheat broiler.

2. Cut tenderloin crosswise into 8 slices. Press each slice with the heal of your hand to form ½-inch thick patties.

3. Combine paprika, salt and red pepper; reserve ¾ teaspoon of paprika mixture. Sprinkle remaining mixture over both sides of tenderloin patties.

4. Broil pork 4 to 5 inches from heat source 4 minutes per side or until pork is barely pink in center.

5. Spoon sauerkraut evenly over patties; spread sour cream over sauerkraut. Sprinkle reserved paprika mixture over sour cream. Return to broiler; broil 1 to 2 minutes or until hot. Garnish with dill and dill sprigs, if desired.   *Makes 4 servings*

NUTRIENTS PER SERVING: Carbohydrate: 5 g, Calories: 165, Fat: 4 g, Protein: 25 g

Poultry Paradise

Roast Chicken with Peppers

   1 cut-up chicken (3 to 3½ pounds)
   3 tablespoons olive oil, divided
1½ tablespoons chopped fresh rosemary *or* 1½ teaspoons dried rosemary, crushed
   1 tablespoon fresh lemon juice
1¼ teaspoons salt, divided
   ¾ teaspoon freshly ground black pepper, divided
   3 bell peppers (preferably 1 red, 1 yellow and 1 green)
   1 medium onion

1. Heat oven to 375°F. Rinse chicken in cold water; pat dry with paper towel. Place in shallow roasting pan.

2. Combine 2 tablespoons of the oil, rosemary and lemon juice; brush over chicken. Sprinkle 1 teaspoon salt and ½ teaspoon pepper over chicken. Roast 15 minutes.

3. Cut bell peppers lengthwise into ½-inch thick strips. Slice onion into thin wedges. Toss vegetables with remaining 1 tablespoon oil, ¼ teaspoon salt and ¼ teaspoon pepper. Spoon vegetables around chicken; roast until vegetables are tender and chicken is cooked through, about 40 minutes. Serve chicken with vegetables and pan juices.

Makes 6 servings

NUTRIENTS PER SERVING: Carbohydrate: 7 g, Calories: 345, Fat: 22 g, Protein: 30 g

Oriental Chicken Kabobs

1 pound boneless skinless chicken breasts
2 small zucchini or yellow squash, cut into 1-inch slices
8 large fresh mushrooms
1 cup red, yellow or green bell pepper pieces
2 tablespoons low sodium soy sauce
2 tablespoons dry sherry
1 teaspoon dark sesame oil
2 cloves garlic, minced
2 large green onions, cut into 1-inch pieces

1. Cut chicken into 1½-inch pieces; place in large plastic bag. Add zucchini, mushrooms and bell pepper to bag. Combine soy sauce, sherry, oil and garlic in cup; pour over chicken and vegetables. Close bag securely; turn to coat. Marinate in refrigerator at least 30 minutes or up to 4 hours.

2. Soak 4 (12-inch) skewers in water to cover 20 minutes.

3. Drain chicken and vegetables; reserve marinade. Alternately thread chicken and vegetables with onions onto skewers.

4. Place on rack of broiler pan. Brush with half of reserved marinade. Broil 5 to 6 inches from heat 5 minutes. Turn kabobs over; brush with remaining marinade. Broil 5 minutes or until chicken is no longer pink. Garnish with green onion brushes, if desired.

Makes 4 servings

NUTRIENTS PER SERVING: Carbohydrate: 6 g, Calories: 135, Fat: 3 g, Protein: 19 g

Oriental Chicken Kabobs

Roasted Rosemary Chicken Legs

¼ **cup finely chopped onion**
 2 **tablespoons margarine or butter, melted**
 1 **tablespoon chopped fresh rosemary** *or* **1 teaspoon dried rosemary**
½ **teaspoon salt**
¼ **teaspoon black pepper**
 2 **cloves garlic, minced**
 4 **chicken legs (about 1½ pounds)**
¼ **cup white wine or chicken broth**

Preheat oven to 375°F.

Combine onion, margarine, rosemary, salt, pepper and garlic in small bowl; set aside. Run finger under skin to loosen. Rub onion mixture under and over skin. Place chicken skin-side up in small shallow roasting pan. Pour wine over chicken.

Roast chicken 50 to 60 minutes or until chicken is browned and juices run clear, basting often with pan juices.   *Makes 4 servings*

NUTRIENTS PER SERVING: Carbohydrate: 2 g, Calories: 263, Fat: 17 g, Protein: 22 g

Roasted Rosemary Chicken Leg

Broiled Chicken Breast with Cilantro Salsa

4 small boneless skinless chicken breast halves (4 ounces each)
4 tablespoons lime juice, divided
   Black pepper
½ cup lightly packed fresh cilantro, chopped
⅓ cup thinly sliced or minced green onions
¼ to ½ jalapeño pepper,* seeded and minced
2 tablespoons pine nuts, toasted (optional)

*Jalapeño peppers can sting and irritate the skin. Wear rubber gloves when handling peppers and do not touch eyes. Wash hands after handling.

1. Spray broiler pan or baking sheet with nonstick cooking spray.

2. Brush chicken with 2 tablespoons lime juice. Place on prepared pan. Sprinkle generously with pepper; set aside.

3. Combine remaining 2 tablespoons lime juice, cilantro, onions, jalapeño pepper and pine nuts, if desired, in small bowl; stir to combine. Set aside.

4. Broil chicken 1 to 2 inches from heat 8 to 10 minutes or until chicken is no longer pink in center. Serve with cilantro salsa. Garnish with lime slices,if desired.

Makes 4 servings

NUTRIENTS PER SERVING: Carbohydrate: 2 g, Calories: 122, Fat: 3 g, Protein: 22 g

Broiled Chicken Breasts with Cilantro Salsa

Persian Chicken Breasts

1 medium lemon
2 teaspoons olive oil
1 teaspoon ground cinnamon
½ teaspoon salt
¼ teaspoon black pepper
¼ teaspoon turmeric
4 boneless skinless chicken breast halves
Grilled vegetables (optional)

1. Remove lemon peel in long strips with paring knife; reserve for garnish. Juice lemon; combine juice with oil, cinnamon, salt, pepper and turmeric in large heavy-duty resealable plastic food storage bag. Gently knead ingredients in bag to mix thoroughly; add chicken. Seal bag and turn to coat thoroughly. Refrigerate 4 hours or overnight.

2. Remove chicken from marinade and gently shake to remove excess. Discard remaining marinade. Grill chicken 5 to 7 minutes per side or until chicken is no longer pink in center. Serve chicken with grilled vegetables, if desired. *Makes 4 servings*

NUTRIENTS PER SERVING: Carbohydrate: 1 g, Calories: 143, Fat: 4 g, Protein: 25 g

Persian Chicken Breasts

Spicy Pistachio Chicken

Prep Time: 10 minutes   *Cook Time:* 40 minutes

4 TYSON® Individually Fresh Frozen® Boneless, Skinless Chicken Breasts
1 tablespoon unsalted butter, melted
¼ teaspoon cayenne pepper
¼ cup finely chopped pistachio nuts
1 tablespoon grated Parmesan cheese
1 tablespoon finely chopped green onion

PREP: Preheat oven to 350°F. Prepare 4 pieces of foil large enough for each to hold 1 chicken breast. CLEAN: Wash hands. Place each breast on piece of foil. Brush chicken with melted butter and sprinkle with pepper. Wrap foil around chicken. CLEAN: Wash hands.

COOK: Place foil packets on cookie sheet; bake 35 minutes. Remove from oven; open foil and sprinkle pistachio nuts over chicken. Leave foil open and return to oven. Bake about 5 minutes or until internal juices of chicken run clear. (Or insert instant-read meat thermometer in thickest part of chicken. Temperature should read 170°F.)

SERVE: Remove chicken from foil and place on serving platter. Sprinkle chicken with Parmesan cheese and green onion.

CHILL: Refrigerate leftovers immediately.   *Makes 4 servings*

NUTRIENTS PER SERVING: Carbohydrate: 2 g, Calories: 220, Fat: 10 g, Protein: 29 g

Italian Turkey Cutlets

1 can (8 ounces) tomato sauce
1 tablespoon CRISCO® Oil*
1½ teaspoons dried oregano leaves
1 tablespoon dried parsley flakes
1 teaspoon dried thyme leaves
½ teaspoon salt
1 clove garlic, minced, *or* ½ teaspoon garlic powder
¼ teaspoon crushed red pepper
1 pound turkey breast cutlets

*Use your favorite Crisco Oil product.

1. Combine tomato sauce, oil, oregano, parsley, thyme, salt, garlic and crushed red pepper in small bowl.

2. Spread one tablespoon sauce over each cutlet. Roll up. Place, seam side down, in 8-inch square baking dish. Spoon remaining sauce over cutlets. Refrigerate at least 30 minutes.

3. Heat oven to 350°F. Place cooling rack on countertop.

4. Bake at 350°F for 25 minutes. *Do not overbake.* Remove baking dish to cooling rack. Serve warm.   *Makes 4 servings*

NUTRIENTS PER SERVING: Carbohydrate: 5 g, Calories: 180, Fat: 5 g, Protein: 28 g

Chicken Rolls Stuffed with Peppers

4 boneless skinless chicken breast halves (about 1¼ pounds)
1 cup water
½ teaspoon onion powder
¼ teaspoon garlic powder
2 cups thin red, yellow *and/or* green bell pepper strips
1½ teaspoons olive oil, divided
¼ teaspoon dried oregano leaves
¼ teaspoon dried thyme leaves
⅛ teaspoon black pepper
1 tablespoon grated Romano cheese
1 tablespoon fine dry bread crumbs

Preheat oven to 350°F. Pound chicken breasts between two sheets of waxed paper with flat side of meat mallet to about ¼-inch thickness. Store chicken in refrigerator until needed.

Combine water, onion powder and garlic powder in small saucepan; bring to a boil over high heat. Add bell peppers; return to a boil. Reduce heat to medium-low. Simmer, covered, 2 to 3 minutes or until bell peppers are crisp-tender. Drain.

Combine ½ teaspoon oil, oregano, thyme and black pepper in small bowl. Spread mixture over one side of flattened chicken breasts; arrange bell peppers on top. Roll up chicken; secure with wooden toothpicks or metal skewers. Place chicken, seam side down, in ungreased 8-inch square baking dish. Brush chicken with remaining 1 teaspoon oil.

Combine Romano cheese and bread crumbs in small cup; sprinkle over chicken. Bake, uncovered, 20 to 25 minutes or until chicken is golden brown and no longer pink in center. Remove toothpicks before serving.   *Makes 4 servings*

NUTRIENTS PER SERVING: Carbohydrate: 9 g, Calories: 209, Fat: 6 g, Protein: 29 g

Chicken Scaloppine with Lemon-Caper Sauce

1 pound boneless skinless chicken breasts
3 tablespoons all-purpose flour, divided
¼ teaspoon black pepper
¼ teaspoon chili powder
½ cup fat-free, reduced-sodium chicken broth
1 tablespoon lemon juice
1 tablespoon drained capers
½ teaspoon olive oil

1. Place chicken breasts, 1 at a time, between sheets of waxed paper. Pound to ¼-inch thickness. Combine 2 tablespoons flour, pepper and chili powder in shallow plate. Dip chicken pieces in flour mixture to lightly coat both sides.

2. Combine broth, lemon juice, remaining flour and capers in small bowl.

3. Spray large skillet with nonstick cooking spray; heat over medium-high heat. Place chicken in hot pan in single layer; cook 1½ minutes. Turn over; cook 1 to 1½ minutes or until chicken is no longer pink in center. Repeat with remaining chicken (brush pan with ¼ teaspoon oil each time you add pieces to prevent sticking). If cooking more than 2 batches, reduce heat to medium to prevent burning chicken.

4. Stir broth mixture and pour into skillet. Boil 1 to 2 minutes or until thickened. Serve immediately over chicken.

Makes 4 servings

NUTRIENTS PER SERVING: Carbohydrate: 4 g, Calories: 144, Fat: 4 g, Protein: 22 g

Chicken Scaloppine with Lemon-Caper Sauce

Roasted Chicken with Maple Glaze

1 (3-pound) broiler-fryer
1 small onion, cut into wedges
1 small orange, cut into wedges
¾ cup apple cider
¼ cup maple syrup
¾ teaspoon cornstarch
¼ teaspoon pumpkin pie spice

Preheat oven to 325°F. Remove giblets and neck from chicken; reserve for another use. Rinse chicken under cold water and pat dry with paper towels.

Place onion and orange wedges in cavity of chicken. Tie legs together with wet cotton string and place breast-side up on rack in shallow roasting pan coated with nonstick cooking spray. Insert meat thermometer into meaty part of thigh not touching bone.

Combine apple cider, maple syrup, cornstarch and pumpkin pie spice in small saucepan, stirring until cornstarch is dissolved. Bring to a boil over medium heat, stirring constantly; cook 1 minute. Brush apple cider mixture over chicken.

Bake chicken 1½ to 2 hours or until meat thermometer registers 180°F, basting frequently with remaining cider mixture.

Remove string from chicken; discard. Remove onion and orange wedges from chicken cavity; discard. Transfer chicken to serving platter. Let stand 10 minutes before carving.

Makes 4 servings

NUTRIENTS PER SERVING: Carbohydrate: 8 g, Calories: 144, Fat: 6 g, Protein: 14 g

Roasted Chicken with Maple Glaze

Lemon Pepper Chicken

⅓ cup lemon juice
¼ cup finely chopped onion
¼ cup olive oil
1 tablespoon brown sugar
1 tablespoon cracked black pepper
3 cloves garlic, minced
2 teaspoons grated lemon peel
¾ teaspoon salt
4 chicken quarters (about 2½ pounds)

Combine lemon juice, onion, oil, sugar, pepper, garlic, lemon peel and salt in small bowl; reserve 2 tablespoons marinade. Combine remaining marinade and chicken in large resealable plastic food storage bag. Seal bag; knead to coat. Refrigerate at least 4 hours or overnight.

Remove chicken from marinade; discard marinade. Arrange chicken on microwavable plate; cover with waxed paper. Microwave at HIGH 5 minutes. Turn and rearrange chicken. Cover and microwave at HIGH 5 minutes.

Transfer chicken to grill. Grill covered over medium-hot coals 15 to 20 minutes or until juices run clear, turning several times and basting often with reserved marinade.

Makes 4 servings

NUTRIENTS PER SERVING: Carbohydrate: 3 g, Calories: 375, Fat: 23 g, Protein: 37 g

Lemon Pepper Chicken

BLT Chicken Salad for Two

2 boneless skinless chicken breast halves
¼ cup mayonnaise or salad dressing
½ teaspoon black pepper
4 large lettuce leaves
1 large tomato, seeded and diced
3 slices crisp-cooked bacon, crumbled
1 hard-cooked egg, sliced
   Additional mayonnaise or salad dressing

1. Brush chicken with mayonnaise; sprinkle with pepper. Grill over hot coals 5 to 7 minutes per side or until no longer pink in center. Cool slightly; cut into thin strips.

2. Arrange lettuce leaves on serving plates. Top with chicken, tomato, bacon and egg. Spoon additional mayonnaise over top.   *Makes 2 servings*

NUTRIENTS PER SERVING: Carbohydrate: 4 g, Calories: 444, Fat: 34 g, Protein: 32 g

BLT Chicken Salad for Two

Chicken Provençal

1 tablespoon olive oil
2 pounds skinless chicken thighs
½ cup sliced green bell pepper
½ cup sliced onion
2 cloves garlic, minced
1 pound eggplant, peeled and cut into ¼-inch-thick slices
2 medium tomatoes, cut into ¼-inch-thick slices
¼ cup chopped fresh parsley *or* 2 teaspoons dried parsley
¼ cup chopped fresh basil *or* 2 teaspoons dried basil leaves
1 teaspoon salt
1 cup fat-free reduced-sodium chicken broth
½ cup dry white wine

Heat oil in large skillet over medium-high heat. Add chicken; cook 2 to 3 minutes on each side or until browned. Remove chicken.

Add bell pepper, onion and garlic to same skillet; cook and stir 3 to 4 minutes or until onion is tender.

Return chicken to skillet. Arrange eggplant and tomato slices over chicken. Sprinkle with parsley, basil and salt. Add chicken broth and wine; bring to a boil. Reduce heat; cover and simmer 45 to 50 minutes or until juices from chicken run clear.   *Makes 6 servings*

NUTRIENTS PER SERVING: Carbohydrate: 10 g, Calories: 216, Fat: 10 g, Protein: 19 g

Japanese Yakitori

1 pound boneless skinless chicken breast halves, cut into ¾-inch-wide strips
2 tablespoons sherry or pineapple juice
2 tablespoons reduced-sodium soy sauce
1 tablespoon sugar
1 tablespoon peanut oil
½ teaspoon minced garlic
½ teaspoon minced ginger
5 ounces red pearl onions
½ fresh pineapple, cut into 1-inch wedges

1. Place chicken in large heavy-duty resealable plastic food storage bag. Combine sherry, soy sauce, sugar, oil, garlic and ginger in small bowl; mix thoroughly to dissolve sugar. Pour into plastic bag with chicken; seal bag and turn to coat thoroughly. Refrigerate 30 minutes or up to 2 hours, turning occasionally. (If using wooden or bamboo skewers, prepare by soaking skewers in water 20 to 30 minutes to keep from burning.)

2. Meanwhile, place onions in boiling water for 4 minutes; drain and cool in ice water to stop cooking. Cut off root ends and slip off outer skins; set aside.

3. Drain chicken, reserving marinade. Weave chicken accordion-style onto skewers, alternating onions and pineapple with chicken. Brush with reserved marinade; discard remaining marinade.

4. Grill on uncovered grill over medium-hot coals 6 to 8 minutes or until chicken is no longer pink in center, turning once.   *Makes 6 servings*

NUTRIENTS PER SERVING: Carbohydrate: 6 g, Calories: 124, Fat: 3 g, Protein: 17 g

Roast Turkey Breast with Spinach-Blue Cheese Stuffing

1 frozen whole boneless turkey breast, thawed (3½ to 4 pounds)
1 package (10 ounces) frozen chopped spinach, thawed and squeezed dry
2 ounces blue cheese or feta cheese
2 ounces reduced-fat cream cheese
½ cup finely chopped green onions
4½ teaspoons Dijon mustard
4½ teaspoons dried basil leaves
2 teaspoons dried oregano leaves
Black pepper to taste
Paprika

1. Preheat oven to 350°F. Coat roasting pan and rack with nonstick cooking spray.

2. Unroll turkey breast; rinse and pat dry. Place between 2 sheets of plastic wrap. Pound turkey breast with flat side of meat mallet to create even piece about 1 inch thick. Remove and discard skin from one half of turkey breast; turn meat over so skin side (on other half) faces down.

3. Combine spinach, blue cheese, cream cheese, green onions, mustard, basil and oregano in medium bowl; mix well. Spread evenly over turkey breast. Roll up turkey so skin is on top.

4. Carefully place turkey breast on rack; sprinkle with pepper and paprika. Roast 1½ hours or until no longer pink in center of breast. Remove from oven and let stand 10 minutes before removing skin and slicing. Cut into ¼-inch slices.

Makes 14 servings (3 ounces each)

NUTRIENTS PER SERVING: Carbohydrate: 2 g, Calories: 135, Fat: 4 g, Protein: 22 g

West Indies Herb & Spice Baked Chicken

Yogurt Mint Sauce (recipe follows)
6 boneless skinless chicken breast halves
1 tablespoon garlic, minced
1 tablespoon lime juice
1 teaspoon olive oil
½ teaspoon dried thyme leaves
½ teaspoon ground nutmeg
½ teaspoon ground cinnamon
½ teaspoon black pepper
½ teaspoon ground allspice
½ teaspoon ground cloves

1. Preheat oven to 400°F. Prepare Yogurt Mint Sauce.

2. Spray jelly-roll pan with nonstick cooking spray. Place breasts on prepared pan. Combine garlic, lime juice, oil, thyme, nutmeg, cinnamon, pepper, allspice and cloves in small bowl; spread evenly over breasts. Bake 15 minutes or until chicken is no longer pink in center. Serve with Yogurt Mint Sauce. *Makes 6 servings*

NUTRIENTS PER SERVING: Carbohydrate: 5 g, Calories: 174, Fat: 4 g, Protein: 28 g

Yogurt Mint Sauce

½ cup plain nonfat yogurt
1 tablespoon brown sugar
1 tablespoon minced fresh mint leaves

1. Combine all ingredients in small bowl; mix well. *Makes ½ cup*

Blue Cheese Stuffed Chicken Breasts

Prep and Cook Time: 22 minutes

  2 tablespoons margarine or butter, softened, divided
½ cup (2 ounces) crumbled blue cheese
¾ teaspoon dried thyme leaves
  2 whole boneless chicken breasts with skin (not split)
  1 tablespoon bottled or fresh lemon juice
½ teaspoon paprika

1. Prepare grill for grilling. Combine 1 tablespoon margarine, blue cheese and thyme in small bowl until blended. Season with salt and pepper.

2. Loosen skin over breast of chicken by pushing fingers between skin and meat, taking care not to tear skin. Spread blue cheese mixture under skin with a rubber spatula or small spoon; massage skin to evenly spread cheese mixture.

3. Place chicken, skin side down, on grid over medium coals. Grill over covered grill 5 minutes. Meanwhile, melt remaining 1 tablespoon margarine; stir in lemon juice and paprika. Turn chicken; brush with lemon juice mixture. Grill 5 to 7 minutes more or until chicken is cooked through. Transfer chicken to carving board; cut each breast in half.

Makes 4 servings

NUTRIENTS PER SERVING: Carbohydrate: 1 g, Calories: 296, Fat: 17 g, Protein: 32 g

Blue Cheese Stuffed Chicken Breast

Fiesta Chicken Thighs

Prep Time: 10 minutes   *Cook Time:* 55 minutes

8 TYSON® Individually Fresh Frozen® Chicken Thighs
¼ cup hot jalapeño jelly
2 tablespoons olive oil
1 tablespoon lime juice
1 teaspoon garlic salt
1 teaspoon lemon pepper
1 teaspoon chili powder

PREP: Preheat oven to 400°F. Line 15×11×1-inch baking pan with foil; spray with nonstick cooking spray. CLEAN: Wash hands. Remove protective ice glaze from frozen chicken by holding under cool running water 1 to 2 minutes. Arrange chicken in single layer in prepared pan. CLEAN: Wash hands.

COOK: Bake 20 minutes; drain and discard juices. In small bowl, combine jelly, oil, lime juice, garlic salt, lemon pepper and chili powder. Turn chicken over and baste with half of sauce. Bake 20 minutes. Turn chicken over and baste with remaining sauce. Bake 10 to 15 minutes or until internal juices of chicken run clear. (Or insert instant-read meat thermometer in thickest part of chicken. Temperature should read 180°F.)

SERVE: Remove chicken and sauce to warm platter. Garnish with lime wedges, if desired.

CHILL: Refrigerate leftovers immediately.   *Makes 8 servings*

NUTRIENTS PER SERVING: Carbohydrate: 8 g, Calories: 440, Fat: 38 g, Protein: 17 g

Chicken Roll-Ups

¼ **cup fresh lemon juice**
1 **tablespoon olive oil**
¼ **teaspoon salt**
¼ **teaspoon black pepper**
4 **boneless skinless chicken breast halves**
¼ **cup finely chopped fresh Italian parsley**
2 **tablespoons grated Parmesan cheese**
2 **tablespoons chopped fresh chives**
1 **teaspoon finely grated lemon peel**
2 **large cloves garlic, pressed in garlic press**
16 **toothpicks soaked in hot water 15 minutes**

1. Combine lemon juice, oil, salt and pepper in 11×7-inch casserole. Pound chicken to ³⁄₈-inch thickness. Place chicken in lemon mixture; turn to coat. Cover; marinate in refrigerator at least 30 minutes.

2. Prepare grill for direct cooking.

3. Combine parsley, cheese, chives, lemon peel and garlic in small bowl. Discard chicken marinade. Spread ¼ of parsley mixture over each chicken breast, leaving an inch around edges free. Starting at narrow end, roll chicken to enclose filling; secure with toothpicks.

4. Grill chicken, covered, over medium-hot coals about 2 minutes on each side or until golden brown. Transfer chicken to low or indirect heat; grill, covered, about 5 minutes or until chicken is no longer pink in center.

5. Remove toothpicks; slice each chicken breast into 3 or 4 pieces.   *Makes 4 servings*

NUTRIENTS PER SERVING: Carbohydrate: 2 g, Calories: 159, Fat: 4 g, Protein: 27 g

Chicken Roll-Up

Turkey with Mustard Sauce

Prep Time: 5 minutes   *Cook Time:* 15 minutes

1 tablespoon butter or margarine
1 pound turkey cutlets
1 cup BIRDS EYE® frozen Mixed Vegetables
1 box (9 ounces) BIRDS EYE® frozen Pearl Onions in Cream Sauce
1 teaspoon spicy brown mustard

• In large nonstick skillet, melt butter over medium-high heat. Add turkey; cook until browned on both sides.

• Add mixed vegetables, onions with cream sauce and mustard; bring to boil. Reduce heat to medium-low; cover and simmer 6 to 8 minutes or until vegetables are tender and turkey is no longer pink in center.   *Makes 4 servings*

Serving Suggestion: Serve with a fresh garden salad.

NUTRIENTS PER SERVING: Carbohydrate: 7 g, Calories: 218, Fat: 5 g, Protein: 35 g

Wish-Bone® Marinade Italiano

¾ cup WISH-BONE® Italian Dressing*
2½ to 3 pounds chicken pieces**

*Also terrific with Wish-Bone® Robusto Italian or Just 2 Good Italian Dressing.

In large, shallow nonaluminum baking dish or plastic bag, pour ½ cup Italian dressing over chicken. Cover, or close bag, and marinate in refrigerator, turning occasionally, 3 to 24 hours.

Remove chicken from marinade; discard marinade. Grill or broil chicken, turning once and brushing frequently with remaining dressing, until chicken is no longer pink.

Makes about 4 servings

**Variations: Use 1 (2- to 2½-pound) T-bone, boneless sirloin or top loin steak or 6 boneless, skinless chicken breast halves (about 1½ pounds) or 2½ pounds center cut pork chops (about 1 inch thick).

NUTRIENTS PER SERVING: Carbohydrate: 2 g, Calories: 410, Fat: 25 g, Protein: 41 g

Chicken Breasts with Orange Basil Pesto

½ cup fresh basil leaves
2 tablespoons grated orange peel
2 cloves garlic
2 teaspoons olive oil
3 tablespoons Florida orange juice
1 tablespoon Dijon-style mustard
  Salt and pepper to taste
6 chicken breast halves

Preheat broiler. Add basil, orange peel and garlic to food processor; process until finely chopped. Add oil, orange juice, mustard, salt and pepper; process a few seconds or until paste forms. Spread equal amounts mixture under skin and on bone side of each chicken breast. Place chicken skin-side down on broiler pan and place 4 inches from heat. Broil 10 minutes. Turn chicken over and broil 10 to 12 minutes or until chicken is no longer pink in center. If chicken browns too quickly, cover with foil. Remove skin from chicken before serving.

Makes 6 servings

Favorite recipe from **Florida Department of Citrus**

NUTRIENTS PER SERVING: Carbohydrate: 3 g, Calories: 206, Fat: 6 g, Protein: 34 g

Chicken Breast with Orange Basil Pesto

Mexican Turkey Tenderloin with Chunky Tomato Sauce

1 teaspoon ground cumin

¾ teaspoon garlic powder

1 pound turkey breast tenderloin, cut into 4 pieces

2 tablespoons vinegar

2 teaspoons sugar

2 teaspoons cornstarch

1 cup coarsely chopped tomatoes

1 cup chopped zucchini

⅓ cup chopped onion

1 tablespoon chopped fresh cilantro *or* 1 teaspoon dried cilantro leaves, crushed

1 tablespoon chopped jalapeño pepper*

Jalapeño peppers can sting and irritate the skin; wear rubber gloves when handling peppers and do not touch eyes. Wash hands after handling peppers.

Preheat broiler. Combine cumin and garlic powder in small bowl; rub mixture on both sides of turkey. Place turkey on broiler pan. Broil 4 inches below heat 5 minutes. Turn and broil about 5 minutes more or until juices run clear and turkey is no longer pink in center.

Meanwhile, combine vinegar, sugar and cornstarch in small saucepan until smooth. Stir in tomatoes, zucchini, onion, cilantro and jalapeño pepper. Cook and stir over medium heat until mixture boils and thickens. Cook and stir 2 minutes more. Spoon over turkey.

Makes 4 servings

NUTRIENTS PER SERVING: Carbohydrate: 9 g, Calories: 151, Fat: 3 g, Protein: 23 g

Chicken-Asparagus Marsala

4 boneless, skinless chicken breast halves
2 tablespoons butter or margarine
1 pound fresh asparagus, cut in 5-inch spears*
½ pound small mushrooms
¼ cup Marsala wine
¼ cup water
½ teaspoon salt
¼ teaspoon pepper
1 tablespoon chopped parsley

*1½ packages (10 ounces each) frozen asparagus spears can be substituted.

On hard surface with meat mallet or similar flattening utensil, pound chicken to ¼-inch thickness. In frypan, place butter or margarine; heat to medium-high temperature. Add chicken and cook, turning, about 5 minutes or until browned. Remove chicken and set aside. To drippings remaining in same frypan, add mushrooms and cook, stirring, about 2 minutes. Add Marsala wine, water, salt and pepper. Return chicken to pan; spoon sauce over chicken. Arrange asparagus over chicken. Heat to boiling; reduce heat to medium, cover and cook about 8 minutes or until chicken is fork tender. Transfer chicken and asparagus to serving platter; keep warm. Heat Marsala sauce to boiling and boil about 2 minutes to reduce liquid. Spoon sauce over chicken; sprinkle with chopped parsley.

Makes 4 servings

Favorite recipe from **Delmarva Poultry Industry, Inc.**

NUTRIENTS PER SERVING: Carbohydrate: 8 g, Calories: 236, Fat: 8 g, Protein: 31 g

Grilled Rosemary Chicken

Prep and Cook Time: 30 minutes

  2 tablespoons lemon juice
  2 tablespoons olive oil
  2 cloves garlic, minced
  2 tablespoons minced fresh rosemary
  ¼ teaspoon salt
  4 boneless skinless chicken breasts

1. Whisk together lemon juice, oil, garlic, rosemary and salt in small bowl. Pour into shallow glass dish. Add chicken, turning to coat both sides with lemon juice mixture. Cover and marinate in refrigerator 15 minutes, turning chicken once.

2. Grill chicken over medium-hot coals 5 to 6 minutes per side or until chicken is no longer pink in center. *Makes 4 servings*

Tip: For added flavor, moisten a few sprigs of fresh rosemary and toss on the hot coals just before grilling. Store rosemary in the refrigerator for up to five days. Wrap sprigs in a barely damp paper towel and place in a sealed plastic bag.

NUTRIENTS PER SERVING: Carbohydrate: <1 g, Calories: 156, Fat: 5 g, Protein: 25 g

Grilled Rosemary Chicken

Balsamic Chicken

6 boneless skinless chicken breast halves
1½ teaspoons fresh rosemary, minced, *or* ½ teaspoon dried rosemary
2 cloves garlic, minced
¾ teaspoon black pepper
½ teaspoon salt
1 tablespoon olive oil
¼ cup good-quality balsamic vinegar

1. Rinse chicken and pat dry. Combine rosemary, garlic, pepper and salt in small bowl; mix well. Place chicken in large bowl; drizzle chicken with oil and rub with spice mixture. Cover and refrigerate overnight.

2. Preheat oven to 450°F. Spray heavy roasting pan or iron skillet with nonstick cooking spray. Place chicken in pan; bake 10 minutes. Turn chicken over, stirring in 3 to 4 tablespoons water if drippings begin to stick to pan.

3. Bake about 10 minutes or until chicken is golden brown and no longer pink in center. If pan is dry, stir in another 1 to 2 tablespoons water to loosen drippings.

4. Drizzle balsamic vinegar over chicken in pan. Transfer chicken to plates. Stir liquid in pan; drizzle over chicken. Garnish, if desired. *Makes 6 servings*

NUTRIENTS PER SERVING: Carbohydrate: 3 g, Calories: 174, Fat: 5 g, Protein: 27 g

Sensational Seafood

Poached Seafood Italiano

1 tablespoon olive or vegetable oil

1 large clove garlic, minced

¼ cup dry white wine or chicken broth

4 (6 ounces) salmon steaks or fillets

1 can (14.5 ounces) CONTADINA® Recipe Ready Diced Tomatoes with Italian Herbs, undrained

2 tablespoons chopped fresh basil (optional)

1. Heat oil in large skillet. Add garlic; sauté 30 seconds. Add wine. Bring to boil.

2. Add salmon; cover. Reduce heat to medium; simmer 6 minutes.

3. Add undrained tomatoes; simmer 2 minutes or until salmon flakes easily when tested with fork. Sprinkle with basil just before serving, if desired.   *Makes 4 servings*

NUTRIENTS PER SERVING: Carbohydrate: 5 g, Calories: 251, Fat: 9 g, Protein: 34 g

Spicy Crabmeat Frittata

Prep and Cook Time: 20 minutes

1 tablespoon olive oil
1 medium green bell pepper, finely chopped
2 cloves garlic, minced
6 eggs
1 can (6½ ounces) lump white crabmeat, drained
¼ teaspoon black pepper
¼ teaspoon salt
¼ teaspoon pepper sauce
1 large ripe plum tomato, seeded and finely chopped

1. Preheat broiler. Heat oil in 10-inch nonstick skillet with oven-safe handle over medium-high heat. Add bell pepper and garlic to skillet; cook 3 minutes or until soft.

2. While bell pepper and garlic cook, beat eggs in medium bowl. Break up large pieces of crabmeat. Add crabmeat, black pepper, salt and pepper sauce to eggs; blend well. Set aside.

3. Add tomato to skillet, cooking and stirring for 1 minute. Add egg mixture to skillet. Reduce heat to medium-low; cook about 7 minutes or until eggs begin to set around edges.

4. Remove pan from burner and place under broiler 6 inches from heat. Broil about 2 minutes or until top of frittata is browned and set. Remove pan from broiler; slide frittata onto serving plate. Serve immediately.   *Makes 4 servings*

Tip: To save time, use bottled minced garlic.

NUTRIENTS PER SERVING: Carbohydrate: 4 g, Calories: 202, Fat: 12 g, Protein: 19 g

Spicy Crabmeat Frittata

Red Snapper Vera Cruz

Prep and Cook Time: 22 minutes

4 red snapper fillets (1 pound)
¼ cup fresh lime juice
1 tablespoon fresh lemon juice
1 teaspoon chili powder
4 green onions with 4 inches of tops, sliced in ½-inch lengths
1 tomato, coarsely chopped
½ cup chopped Anaheim or green bell pepper
½ cup chopped red bell pepper

1. Place red snapper in shallow round microwavable baking dish. Combine lime juice, lemon juice and chili powder. Pour over snapper. Marinate 10 minutes, turning once or twice.

2. Sprinkle green onions, tomato and peppers over snapper. Cover dish loosely with vented plastic wrap. Microwave at HIGH 6 minutes or just until snapper flakes in center, rotating dish every 2 minutes. Let stand, covered, 4 minutes.   *Makes 4 servings*

NUTRIENTS PER SERVING: Carbohydrate: 7 g, Calories: 144, Fat: 2 g, Protein: 24 g

Red Snapper Vera Cruz

Shrimp Creole Stew

Prep Time: 5 minutes   *Cook Time:* 20 minutes

1½ **cups raw small shrimp, shelled**
  1 **bag (16 ounces) BIRDS EYE® frozen Farm Fresh Mixtures Broccoli, Cauliflower &**
     Red Peppers
  1 **can (14½ ounces) diced tomatoes**
1½ **teaspoons salt**
  1 **teaspoon hot pepper sauce**
  1 **teaspoon vegetable oil**

• In large saucepan, combine all ingredients.

• Cover; bring to boil. Reduce heat to medium-low; simmer 20 minutes or until shrimp turn opaque.   *Makes 4 servings*

NUTRIENTS PER SERVING: Carbohydrate: 9 g, Calories: 131, Fat: 1 g, Protein: 20 g

Shrimp Creole Stew

Seafood Kabobs

Nonstick cooking spray
1 pound uncooked large shrimp, peeled and deveined
10 ounces skinless swordfish or halibut steaks, cut 1 inch thick
2 tablespoons honey mustard
2 teaspoons fresh lemon juice
8 metal skewers (12 inches long)
8 slices bacon (regular slice, not thick)
Lemon wedges and fresh herbs (optional)

1. Spray grid with nonstick cooking spray. Prepare grill for direct cooking.

2. Place shrimp in shallow glass dish. Cut swordfish into 1-inch cubes; add to dish. Combine mustard and lemon juice in small bowl. Pour over shrimp mixture; toss lightly to coat.

3. Pierce one 12-inch metal skewer through 1 end of bacon slice. Add 1 piece shrimp. Pierce skewer through bacon slice again, wrapping bacon slice around 1 side of shrimp.

4. Add 1 piece swordfish. Pierce bacon slice again, wrapping bacon around opposite side of swordfish. Continue adding seafood and wrapping with bacon, pushing ingredients to middle of skewer until end of bacon slice is reached. Repeat with 7 more skewers. Brush any remaining mustard mixture over skewers.

5. Place skewers on grid. Grill, covered, over medium heat 8 to 10 minutes or until shrimp are opaque and swordfish flakes easily when tested with fork, turning halfway through grilling time. Garnish with lemon wedges and fresh herbs, if desired.

Makes 4 servings (2 kabobs per serving)

Note: Kabobs can be prepared up to 3 hours before grilling. Cover and refrigerate until ready to grill.

NUTRIENTS PER SERVING: Carbohydrate: 5 g, Calories: 268, Fat: 10 g, Protein: 37 g

Red Snapper Scampi

Prep and Cook Time: 12 minutes

¼ **cup margarine or butter, softened**
1 **tablespoon white wine**
1½ **teaspoons minced garlic**
½ **teaspoon grated lemon peel**
⅛ **teaspoon black pepper**
1½ **pounds red snapper, orange roughy or grouper fillets (about 4 to 5 ounces each)**

1. Preheat oven to 450°F. Combine margarine, wine, garlic, lemon peel and pepper in small bowl; stir to blend.

2. Place fish on foil-lined shallow baking pan. Top with seasoned margarine. Bake 10 to 12 minutes or until fish begins to flake easily when tested with fork.   *Makes 4 servings*

Tip: Serve fish over mixed salad greens, if desired. Or, add sliced carrots, zucchini and bell pepper cut into matchstick-size strips to the fish in the baking pan for an easy vegetable side dish.

NUTRIENTS PER SERVING: Carbohydrate: 1 g, Calories: 278, Fat: 14 g, Protein: 35 g

Microwaved Lemon-Apple Fish Rolls

4 sole, cod or red snapper fillets (1 pound)
  Grated peel of 1 SUNKIST® lemon, divided
1 teaspoon dried dill weed, divided
¾ cup plus 2 tablespoons apple juice, divided
  Juice of ½ SUNKIST® lemon
2 tablespoons finely minced onion
1 tablespoon unsalted margarine
1 tablespoon all-purpose flour
1 tablespoon chopped parsley

Sprinkle fish with half the lemon peel and half the dill. Roll up each fillet; place, seam-side-down, in 8-inch round microwavable dish. Combine ¾ cup apple juice, lemon juice, onion, remaining lemon peel and dill; pour over fish. Dot with margarine. Cover with vented plastic wrap. Microwave at HIGH 3 minutes. Uncover; spoon cooking liquid over fish. Cook, covered, 3 to 4 minutes or until fish flakes easily with fork. Let stand, covered, while making sauce.

Pour cooking liquid from fish into small microwavable bowl. Blend remaining 2 tablespoons apple juice into flour; stir into cooking liquid. Microwave at HIGH 3 to 4 minutes; stir twice until sauce boils and slightly thickens. Add parsley; spoon over fish.   *Makes 4 servings*

NUTRIENTS PER SERVING: Carbohydrate: 9 g, Calories: 167, Fat: 4 g, Protein: 22 g

Halibut with Cilantro and Lime

1 pound halibut, tuna or swordfish steaks
2 tablespoons fresh lime juice
¼ cup reduced-sodium soy sauce
1 teaspoon cornstarch
½ teaspoon minced fresh ginger
½ teaspoon vegetable oil
½ cup slivered red or yellow onion
2 cloves garlic, minced
¼ cup coarsely chopped fresh cilantro
Lime wedges (optional)

1. Cut halibut into 1-inch pieces; sprinkle with lime juice.

2. Place soy sauce and cornstarch in cup; blend until smooth. Stir in ginger; set aside.

3. Heat oil in wok or large nonstick skillet over medium heat until hot. Add onion and garlic; stir-fry 2 minutes. Add halibut; stir-fry 2 minutes or until fish flakes easily when tested with fork.

4. Stir soy sauce mixture; add to wok. Stir-fry 30 seconds or until sauce boils and thickens. Sprinkle with cilantro. Garnish with lime wedges, if desired.   *Makes 4 servings*

NUTRIENTS PER SERVING: Carbohydrate: 5 g, Calories: 154, Fat: 3 g, Protein: 25 g

Halibut with Cilantro and Lime

Dilled Salmon in Parchment

Prep and Cook Time: 20 minutes

2 skinless salmon fillets (4 to 6 ounces each)
2 tablespoons butter or margarine, melted
1 tablespoon lemon juice
1 tablespoon chopped fresh dill
1 tablespoon chopped shallots

1. Preheat oven to 400°F. Cut 2 pieces parchment paper into 12-inch squares; fold squares in half diagonally and cut into half heart shapes. Open parchment; place fish fillet on one side of each heart.

2. Combine butter and lemon juice in small cup; drizzle over fish. Sprinkle with dill, shallots and salt and pepper to taste.

3. Fold parchment hearts in half. Beginning at top of heart, fold edges together, 2 inches at a time. At tip of heart, fold parchment over to seal.

4. Bake fish about 10 minutes or until parchment pouch puffs up. To serve, cut an "X" through top layer of parchment and fold back points to display contents.

Makes 2 servings

NUTRIENTS PER SERVING: Carbohydrate: 2 g, Calories: 234, Fat: 15 g, Protein: 22 g

Garlic Clams

2 pounds littleneck clams
2 teaspoons olive oil
2 tablespoons finely chopped onion
2 tablespoons chopped garlic
½ cup dry white wine
¼ cup chopped red bell pepper
2 tablespoons lemon juice
1 tablespoon chopped fresh parsley

1. Discard any clams that remain open when tapped with fingers. To clean clams, scrub with stiff brush under cold running water. Soak clams in mixture of ½ cup salt to 1 gallon water 20 minutes. Drain water; repeat 2 more times.

2. Heat oil in large saucepan over medium-high heat until hot. Add onion and garlic; cook and stir about 3 minutes or until garlic is tender but not brown. Add clams, wine, bell pepper and lemon juice. Cover; simmer 3 to 10 minutes or until clams open. Transfer clams as they open to large bowl; cover. Discard any clams that do not open. Increase heat to high. Add parsley; boil until liquid reduces to ¼ to ⅓ cup. Pour over clams; serve immediately. Garnish with parsley sprigs, if desired.   *Makes 4 servings*

NUTRIENTS PER SERVING: Carbohydrate: 5 g, Calories: 107, Fat: 3 g, Protein: 10 g

Garlic Clams

Pineapple Salsa Topped Halibut

Pineapple Salsa

¾ cup diced fresh pineapple *or* 1 can (8 ounces) unsweetened pineapple tidbits, drained

2 tablespoons finely chopped red bell pepper

2 tablespoons chopped fresh cilantro

2 teaspoons vegetable oil

1 teaspoon bottled minced ginger or finely shredded fresh ginger

1 teaspoon bottled minced jalapeño pepper or fresh jalapeño pepper*

Halibut

4 halibut or swordfish steaks (6 ounces each), cut about ¾-inch thick

1 tablespoon garlic-flavored olive oil**

¼ teaspoon salt

Jalapeño peppers can sting and irritate the skin; wear rubber gloves when handling peppers and do not touch eyes. Wash hands after handling.

**Or, add ¼ teaspoon bottled minced garlic to 1 tablespoon olive oil.*

1. For salsa, combine pineapple, bell pepper, cilantro, oil, ginger and jalapeño pepper in small bowl; mix well.

2. Prepare barbecue grill for direct cooking. Brush halibut with oil; sprinkle with salt.

3. Grill halibut, on uncovered grill, over medium-hot coals 8 minutes or until halibut flakes easily when tested with fork, turning once.

4. Top halibut with salsa; serve immediately.   *Makes 4 servings*

NUTRIENTS PER SERVING: Carbohydrate: 4 g, Calories: 253, Fat: 10 g, Protein: 36 g

Grilled Five-Spice Fish with Garlic Spinach

1½ teaspoons finely shredded lime peel
3 tablespoons fresh lime juice
4 teaspoons minced fresh ginger
½ to 1 teaspoon Chinese 5-spice powder
½ teaspoon sugar
½ teaspoon salt
⅛ teaspoon black pepper
2 teaspoons vegetable oil, divided
1 pound salmon steaks
½ pound fresh baby spinach leaves (about 8 cups lightly packed), washed
2 large cloves garlic, pressed through garlic press

1. Combine lime peel, lime juice, ginger, 5-spice powder, sugar, salt, pepper and 1 teaspoon oil in 2-quart dish. Add salmon; turn to coat. Cover and refrigerate 2 to 3 hours.

2. Combine spinach, garlic and remaining 1 teaspoon oil in medium microwaveable dish; toss. Cover and microwave at HIGH (100% power) 2 minutes or until spinach is wilted. Drain; keep warm.

3. Meanwhile, prepare barbecue grill for direct cooking.

4. Remove salmon from marinade and place on oiled grid. Brush salmon with portion of marinade. Grill salmon, covered, over medium-hot coals 4 minutes. Turn salmon; brush with marinade and grill 4 minutes or until salmon flakes easily with fork. Discard marinade.

5. Serve fish over bed of spinach.

Makes 4 servings

NUTRIENTS PER SERVING: Carbohydrate: 4 g, Calories: 133, Fat: 3 g, Protein: 22 g

Grilled Five-Spice Fish with Garlic Spinach

Garlic Skewered Shrimp

1 pound large shrimp, peeled and deveined
2 tablespoons reduced-sodium soy sauce
1 tablespoon vegetable oil
3 cloves garlic, minced
¼ teaspoon red pepper flakes (optional)
3 green onions, cut into 1-inch pieces

Prepare grill or preheat broiler. Soak 4 (12-inch) skewers in water 20 minutes. Meanwhile, place shrimp in large plastic bag. Combine soy sauce, oil, garlic and red pepper in cup; mix well. Pour over shrimp. Close bag securely; turn to coat. Marinate at room temperature 15 minutes.

Drain shrimp; reserve marinade. Alternately thread shrimp and onions onto skewers. Place skewers on grid or rack of broiler pan. Brush with reserved marinade; discard any remaining marinade. Grill, covered, over medium-hot coals or broil 5 to 6 inches from heat 5 minutes on each side or until shrimp are pink and opaque. Serve on lettuce-lined plate.

Makes 4 servings

Tip: For a more attractive presentation, leave the tails on the shrimp.

NUTRIENTS PER SERVING: Carbohydrate: 2 g, Calories: 128, Fat: 4 g, Protein: 20 g

Garlic Skewered Shrimp

Roast Dilled Scrod with Asparagus

1 bunch (12 ounces) asparagus spears, ends trimmed
1 teaspoon olive oil
4 (5-ounce) scrod or cod fish fillets
1 tablespoon lemon juice
1 teaspoon dill weed
½ teaspoon salt
¼ teaspoon black pepper
Paprika (optional)

1. Heat oven to 425°F.

2. Place asparagus in 13×9-inch baking dish. Drizzle oil over asparagus. Roll asparagus to coat lightly with oil; push to edges of dish, stacking asparagus into two layers.

3. Arrange fish fillets in center of dish. Drizzle lemon juice over fish. Combine dill weed, salt and pepper; sprinkle over fish and asparagus.

4. Roast in oven 15 to 17 minutes or until fish is opaque in center and asparagus are crisp-tender.   *Makes 4 servings*

NUTRIENTS PER SERVING: Carbohydrate: 4 g, Calories: 147, Fat: 2 g, Protein: 27 g

Baked Fish with Tomatoes & Herbs

1 pound lean white fish fillets, such as orange roughy or sole
2 tablespoons plus 2 teaspoons lemon juice, divided
½ teaspoon paprika
1 cup seeded, finely chopped tomatoes
2 tablespoons capers, rinsed and drained
2 tablespoons finely chopped fresh parsley
1½ teaspoons dried basil leaves
2 teaspoons olive oil
¼ teaspoon salt

1. Preheat oven 350°F. Coat 12×8-inch glass baking pan with nonstick cooking spray.

2. Arrange fish fillets in pan; drizzle 2 tablespoons lemon juice over fillets and sprinkle with paprika. Cover with foil; bake 18 minutes or until opaque in center and flakes easily when tested with fork.

3. Meanwhile, in medium saucepan, combine tomatoes, capers, parsley, remaining 2 teaspoons lemon juice, basil, oil and salt. Five minutes before fish is done, place saucepan over high heat. Bring to a boil. Reduce heat and simmer 2 minutes or until hot. Remove from heat.

4. Serve fish topped with tomato mixture.   *Makes 4 servings*

NUTRIENTS PER SERVING: Carbohydrate: 4 g, Calories: 150, Fat: 4 g, Protein: 24 g

Oriental Baked Cod

2 tablespoons reduced-sodium soy sauce
2 tablespoons apple juice
1 tablespoon finely chopped fresh ginger
2 cloves garlic, minced
1 teaspoon crushed Szechuan peppercorns
4 cod fillets (about 1 pound)
4 green onions, thinly sliced

1. Preheat oven to 375°F. Spray roasting pan with nonstick cooking spray. Combine soy sauce, apple juice, ginger, garlic and Szechuan peppercorns in small bowl; mix well.

2. Place cod fillets in prepared pan; pour soy sauce mixture over fish. Bake about 10 minutes or until fish is opaque and flakes easily when tested with fork.

3. Transfer fish to serving dish; pour pan juices over fish and sprinkle with green onions. Garnish, if desired.   *Makes 4 servings*

NUTRIENTS PER SERVING: Carbohydrate: 3 g, Calories: 100, Fat: 1 g, Protein: 20 g

Oriental Baked Cod

Maryland Crab Cakes

  1 pound fresh backfin crabmeat, cartilage removed
10 low-salt crackers (2 inches each), crushed to equal ½ cup crumbs
  1 rib celery, finely chopped
  1 green onion, finely chopped
  ¼ cup cholesterol-free egg substitute
  3 tablespoons nonfat tartar sauce
  1 teaspoon seafood seasoning
  2 teaspoons vegetable oil

1. Combine crabmeat, cracker crumbs, celery and onion in medium bowl; set aside.

2. Mix egg substitute, tartar sauce and seafood seasoning in small bowl; pour over crabmeat mixture. Gently mix so large lumps will not be broken. Shape into six ¾-inch-thick patties. Cover; refrigerate 30 minutes.

3. Spray skillet with nonstick cooking spray. Add oil; heat over medium-high heat. Place crab cakes in skillet; cook 3 to 4 minutes each side or until cakes are lightly browned. Garnish with lemon wedges, if desired.   *Makes 6 servings*

NUTRIENTS PER SERVING: Carbohydrate: 8 g, Calories: 127, Fat: 4 g, Protein: 14 g

Maryland Crab Cakes

Lemon-Poached Halibut with Carrots

    3 medium carrots, cut into julienne strips
    ¾ cup water
    ¼ cup dry white wine
    2 tablespoons lemon juice
    1 teaspoon dried rosemary
    1 teaspoon dried marjoram leaves
    1 teaspoon chicken or fish bouillon granules
    ¼ teaspoon black pepper
    4 fresh or frozen halibut steaks, cut 1 inch thick (about 1½ pounds)
    ½ cup sliced green onions
       Lemon slices for garnish (optional)

Combine carrots, water, wine, lemon juice, rosemary, marjoram, bouillon granules and pepper in large skillet. Bring to a boil over high heat. Carefully place fish and onions in skillet. Return just to a boil. Reduce heat to medium-low. Cover; simmer 8 to 10 minutes or until fish flakes easily when tested with fork.

Carefully transfer fish to serving platter with slotted spatula. Spoon vegetables over fish. Garnish with lemon slices, if desired. *Makes 4 servings*

NUTRIENTS PER SERVING: Carbohydrate: 8 g, Calories: 224, Fat: 4 g, Protein: 36 g

Lemon-Poached Halibut with Carrots

Herbed Scallops and Shrimp

¼ **cup chopped fresh parsley**
¼ **cup lime juice**
 2 **tablespoons chopped fresh mint**
 2 **tablespoons chopped fresh rosemary**
 1 **tablespoon olive oil**
 1 **tablespoon honey**
 2 **cloves garlic, minced**
¼ **teaspoon black pepper**
½ **pound raw jumbo shrimp, peeled and deveined**
½ **pound bay or halved sea scallops**

1. Preheat broiler. Combine parsley, lime juice, mint, rosemary, oil, honey, garlic and black pepper in medium bowl; blend well. Add shrimp and scallops. Cover; refrigerate 1 hour.

2. Arrange shrimp and scallops on skewers. Place on broiler pan. Brush with marinade. Broil 5 to 6 minutes or until shrimp are opaque and scallops are lightly browned. Serve immediately with lime slices and fresh mint sprigs, if desired.   *Makes 4 servings*

NUTRIENTS PER SERVING: Carbohydrate: 8 g, Calories: 152, Fat: 5 g, Protein: 20 g

Herbed Scallops and Shrimp

Beijing Fillet of Sole

2 tablespoons reduced-sodium soy sauce
2 teaspoons dark sesame oil
4 sole fillets (6 ounces each)
1¼ cups preshredded cabbage or coleslaw mix
½ cup crushed chow mein noodles
1 egg white, slightly beaten
2 teaspoons sesame seeds
1 package (10 ounces) frozen snow peas, cooked and drained

1. Heat oven to 350°F. Combine soy sauce and oil in small bowl. Place sole in shallow dish. Lightly brush both sides of sole with soy mixture.

2. Combine cabbage, crushed noodles, egg white and remaining soy mixture in small bowl. Spoon evenly over sole. Roll up each fillet and place, seam side down, in shallow foil-lined roasting pan.

3. Sprinkle rolls with sesame seeds. Bake 25 to 30 minutes until fish flakes when tested with fork. Serve with snow peas. *Makes 4 servings*

NUTRIENTS PER SERVING: Carbohydrate: 6 g, Calories: 252, Fat: 8 g, Protein: 34 g

Beijing Fillet of Sole

Mustard-Grilled Red Snapper

½ cup Dijon mustard
1 tablespoon red wine vinegar
1 teaspoon ground red pepper
4 red snapper fillets (about 6 ounces each)
Fresh parsley sprigs and red peppercorns (optional)

Spray grid with nonstick cooking spray. Prepare grill for direct cooking. Combine mustard, vinegar and pepper in small bowl; mix well. Coat fish thoroughly with mustard mixture. Place fish on grid. Grill, covered, over medium-high heat 8 minutes or until fish flakes easily when tested with fork, turning halfway through grilling time. Garnish with parsley sprigs and red peppercorns, if desired. *Makes 4 servings*

NUTRIENTS PER SERVING: Carbohydrate: 4 g, Calories: 210, Fat: 5 g, Protein: 37 g

Mustard-Grilled Red Snapper

Broiled Shrimp Skewers

Prep and Cook Time: 20 minutes

> 2 tablespoons olive oil
> 2 tablespoons lemon juice
> ½ teaspoon minced garlic
> ½ teaspoon salt
> ½ teaspoon dried oregano leaves
> ⅛ teaspoon ground red pepper
> ½ pound medium shrimp, peeled
> 1 red bell pepper, cut into 1-inch pieces
> 1 medium zucchini, cut into ½-inch slices

1. Preheat broiler. Whisk together oil, lemon juice, garlic, salt, oregano and ground red pepper in medium bowl. Add shrimp, bell pepper and zucchini; stir until well coated.

2. Alternately thread shrimp, bell pepper and zucchini on skewers. Place on rack of broiler pan. Broil 4 inches from heat 2 minutes per side or until shrimp turns pink and opaque.

Makes 4 servings

NUTRIENTS PER SERVING: Carbohydrate: 6 g, Calories: 131, Fat: 7 g, Protein: 11 g

Skillet Fish with Lemon Tarragon "Butter"

2 teaspoons light margarine
4 teaspoons lemon juice, divided
½ teaspoon grated lemon peel
¼ teaspoon prepared mustard
¼ teaspoon dried tarragon leaves
⅛ teaspoon salt
2 (4-ounce) lean white fish fillets,* rinsed and patted dry
¼ teaspoon paprika
   Nonstick cooking spray

Cod, orange roughy, flounder, haddock, halibut and sole may be used.

1. Combine margarine, 2 teaspoons lemon juice, lemon peel, mustard, tarragon and salt in small bowl. Blend well with fork; set aside.

2. Coat 12-inch nonstick skillet with cooking spray. Heat over medium heat until hot.

3. Drizzle fillets with remaining 2 teaspoons lemon juice. Sprinkle one side of each fillet with paprika. Place fillets in skillet, paprika side down; cook 3 minutes. Gently turn and cook 3 minutes longer or until opaque in center. Place fillets on serving plates; top with margarine mixture.   *Makes 2 servings*

NUTRIENTS PER SERVING: Carbohydrate: 1 g, Calories: 125, Fat: 3 g, Protein: 22 g

Baked Fish with Fresh Mediterranean Salsa

4 (6-ounce) lean, mild fish fillets, such as flounder, tilapia or snapper
2 tablespoons water
½ teaspoon chili powder
1 large tomato, seeded and chopped
1 can (2½ ounces) sliced ripe olives or kalamata olives, drained
2 tablespoons chopped fresh parsley
2 tablespoons lemon juice
1 tablespoon capers, drained
2 teaspoons extra-virgin olive oil
1 teaspoon dried oregano leaves

Preheat oven 350°F. Coat 12×8-inch glass baking dish with nonstick cooking spray; arrange fillets in single layer. Pour water over fillets and sprinkle with chili powder. Cover tightly with aluminum foil and bake 15 minutes or until fish is opaque in center.

Meanwhile, combine tomato, olives, parsley, lemon juice, capers, oil and oregano in small bowl; mix well. Remove fish from pan with slotted spatula and place on individual plates; spoon ⅓ cup salsa over each serving.   *Makes 4 servings*

NUTRIENTS PER SERVING: Carbohydrate: 5 g, Calories: 212, Fat: 6 g, Protein: 33 g

Baked Fish with Fresh Mediterranean Salsa

Grilled Salmon Fillets, Asparagus and Onions

Prep and Cook Time: 26 minutes

½ **teaspoon paprika**
6 **salmon fillets (6 to 8 ounces each)**
⅓ **cup bottled honey-Dijon marinade or barbecue sauce**
1 **bunch (about 1 pound) fresh asparagus spears, ends trimmed**
1 **large red or sweet onion, cut into ¼-inch slices**
1 **tablespoon olive oil**
   Salt and black pepper

1. Prepare grill for direct grilling. Sprinkle paprika over salmon fillets. Brush marinade over salmon; let stand at room temperature 15 minutes.

2. Brush asparagus and onion slices with olive oil; season to taste with salt and pepper.

3. Place salmon, skin side down, in center of grid over medium coals. Arrange asparagus spears and onion slices around salmon. Grill salmon and vegetables on covered grill 5 minutes. Turn salmon, asparagus and onion slices. Grill 5 to 6 minutes more or until salmon flakes easily when tested with a fork and vegetables are crisp-tender. Separate onion slices into rings; arrange over asparagus. *Makes 6 servings*

NUTRIENTS PER SERVING: Carbohydrate: 8 g, Calories: 255, Fat: 8 g, Protein: 35 g

Grilled Salmon Fillet, Asparagus and Onions

Satisfying Salads

Raspberry Mango Salad

 2 cups arugula
 1 cup torn Bibb or Boston lettuce
 ½ cup watercress, stems removed
 1 cup diced mango
 ¾ cup fresh raspberries
 ¼ cup (1½ ounces) crumbled blue cheese
 1 tablespoon olive oil
 1 tablespoon water
 1 tablespoon raspberry vinegar
 ⅛ teaspoon salt
 ⅛ teaspoon black pepper

1. Combine arugula, lettuce, watercress, mango, raspberries and cheese in medium bowl.

2. Shake remaining ingredients in small jar. Pour over salad; toss to coat. Serve immediately. *Makes 4 servings*

NUTRIENTS PER SERVING: Carbohydrate: 4 g, Calories: 98, Fat: 8 g, Protein: 3 g

Grilled Beef Salad

½ cup mayonnaise

2 tablespoons cider vinegar or white wine vinegar

1 tablespoon spicy brown mustard

2 cloves garlic, minced

½ teaspoon sugar

6 cups torn assorted lettuces such as romaine, red leaf and Bibb

1 large tomato, seeded and chopped

⅓ cup chopped fresh basil

2 slices red onion, separated into rings

1 pound boneless beef top sirloin steak, cut 1 inch thick

½ teaspoon salt

½ teaspoon black pepper

½ cup herb or garlic croutons

Additional black pepper (optional)

Prepare grill for direct cooking. Combine mayonnaise, vinegar, mustard, garlic and sugar in small bowl; mix well. Cover and refrigerate until serving.

Toss together lettuce, tomato, basil and onion in large bowl; cover and refrigerate until serving.

Sprinkle both sides of steak with salt and ½ teaspoon pepper. Place steak on grid. Grill, covered, over medium-high heat 10 minutes for medium-rare or until desired doneness is reached, turning halfway through grilling time.

Transfer steak to carving board. Slice in half lengthwise; carve crosswise into thin slices.

Add steak and croutons to bowl with lettuce mixture; toss well. Add mayonnaise mixture; toss until well coated. Serve with additional pepper, if desired. *Makes 4 servings*

NUTRIENTS PER SERVING: Carbohydrate: 8 g, Calories: 383, Fat: 30 g, Protein: 25 g

Grilled Beef Salad

Crab Cobb Salad

12 cups washed and torn romaine lettuce
2 cans (6 ounces each) crabmeat, drained
2 cups diced ripe tomatoes or halved cherry tomatoes
¼ cup (1½ ounces) crumbled blue or Gorgonzola cheese
¼ cup cholesterol-free bacon bits
¾ cup fat-free Italian or Caesar salad dressing
Black pepper

1. Arrange lettuce on large serving platter. Arrange crabmeat, tomatoes, blue cheese and bacon bits in rows attractively over lettuce.

2. Just before serving, drizzle dressing evenly over salad; toss well. Transfer to 8 chilled serving plates; sprinkle with pepper to taste. *Makes 8 servings*

NUTRIENTS PER SERVING: Carbohydrate: 8 g, Calories: 110, Fat: 3 g, Protein: 12 g

Cucumber Salad

2 cucumbers
½ cup plain nonfat yogurt
1 teaspoon dried mint
½ teaspoon sugar

Slice cucumbers. Combine yogurt, mint and sugar in small bowl. Toss cucumbers in yogurt mixture. Serve immediately. *Makes 4 servings*

Favorite recipe from **The Sugar Association, Inc.**

NUTRIENTS PER SERVING: Carbohydrate: 7 g, Calories: 37, Fat: <1 g, Protein: 2 g

Crab Cobb Salad

Grilled Chicken au Poivre Salad

4 boneless skinless chicken breasts (about 1¼ pounds)
¼ cup plus 3 tablespoons olive oil, divided
¼ cup finely chopped onion
2½ tablespoons white wine vinegar, divided
2 teaspoons cracked or coarse ground black pepper
½ teaspoon salt
¼ teaspoon poultry seasoning
3 cloves garlic, minced
1 tablespoon Dijon mustard
Dash sugar
1 bag (10 ounces) prewashed salad greens
2 cherry tomatoes, halved

1. Place chicken, ¼ cup oil, onion, 1 tablespoon vinegar, pepper, salt, poultry seasoning and garlic in large resealable plastic food storage bag. Seal bag; knead to coat chicken. Refrigerate at least 2 hours or overnight.

2. Grill chicken on covered grill over medium-hot coals 10 to 15 minutes or until chicken is no longer pink in center.

3. Combine remaining 3 tablespoons oil, 1½ tablespoons vinegar, mustard and sugar in small bowl; whisk until smooth.

4. Arrange salad greens and cherry tomatoes on 4 plates.

5. Cut chicken crosswise into strips. Arrange strips on top of greens. Drizzle with dressing.

Makes 4 servings

NUTRIENTS PER SERVING: Carbohydrate: 5 g, Calories: 252, Fat: 15 g, Protein: 23 g

Grilled Chicken au Poivre Salad

Easy Greek Salad

Prep Time: 10 minutes

> **6 leaves Romaine lettuce, torn into 1½-inch pieces**
> **1 cucumber, peeled and sliced**
> **1 tomato, chopped**
> **½ cup sliced red onion**
> **1 ounce feta cheese, crumbled (about ⅓ cup)**
> **2 tablespoons extra-virgin olive oil**
> **2 tablespoons lemon juice**
> **1 teaspoon dried oregano leaves**
> **½ teaspoon salt**

1. Combine lettuce, cucumber, tomato, onion and cheese in large serving bowl.

2. Whisk together oil, lemon juice, oregano and salt in small bowl. Pour over lettuce mixture; toss until coated. Serve immediately.   *Makes 6 servings*

Serving Suggestion: This simple but delicious salad makes a great accompaniment for grilled steaks or chicken.

NUTRIENTS PER SERVING: Carbohydrate: 5 g, Calories: 72, Fat: 6 g, Protein: 2 g

Easy Greek Salad

Warm Roasted Vegetable Salad

4 cups broccoli florets
2 red bell peppers, cut into ¼-inch-thick slices
1 small red onion, cut into ¼-inch-thick slices
1 small yellow onion, cut into ¼-inch-thick slices
1½ teaspoons olive oil
1 tablespoon Dijon mustard
1 tablespoon balsamic vinegar
1 teaspoon hot pepper sauce
½ teaspoon salt
¼ cup slivered fresh basil

1. Preheat oven to 350°F. Combine broccoli, bell peppers, onions and oil in large casserole dish; toss to coat.

2. Bake vegetables 25 minutes, stirring occasionally.

3. Meanwhile, combine mustard, vinegar, hot pepper sauce and salt in small bowl with wire whisk until smooth. Stir mixture into hot vegetables; toss to coat. Sprinkle salad with basil; garnish, if desired. Serve warm.   *Makes 6 servings*

NUTRIENTS PER SERVING: Carbohydrate: 8 g, Calories: 50, Fat: 2 g, Protein: 3 g

Warm Roasted Vegetable Salad

Scallop and Spinach Salad

1 package (10 ounces) spinach leaves, washed, stemmed and torn
3 thin slices red onion, halved and separated
12 ounces sea scallops
   Ground red pepper
   Paprika
   Nonstick cooking spray
½ cup prepared fat-free Italian salad dressing
¼ cup crumbled blue cheese
2 tablespoons toasted walnuts

1. Pat spinach dry; place in large bowl with red onion. Cover; set aside.

2. Rinse scallops. Cut in half horizontally (to make 2 thin rounds); pat dry. Sprinkle top side lightly with red pepper and paprika. Spray large nonstick skillet with cooking spray; heat over high heat until very hot. Add half of scallops, seasoned side down, in single layer, placing ½ inch or more apart. Sprinkle with red pepper and paprika. Cook 2 minutes or until browned on bottom. Turn scallops; cook 1 to 2 minutes or until opaque in center. Transfer to plate; cover to keep warm. Wipe skillet clean; repeat procedure with remaining scallops.

3. Place dressing in small saucepan; bring to a boil over high heat. Pour dressing over spinach and onion; toss to coat. Divide among 4 plates. Place scallops on top of spinach; sprinkle with blue cheese and walnuts.   *Makes 4 servings*

NUTRIENTS PER SERVING: Carbohydrate: 6 g, Calories: 169, Fat: 6 g, Protein: 24 g

Scallop and Spinach Salad

Chicken Salad

¼ cup mayonnaise
¼ cup sour cream
1 tablespoon lemon juice
1 teaspoon sugar
1 teaspoon grated lemon peel
1 teaspoon Dijon mustard
½ teaspoon salt
⅛ to ¼ teaspoon white pepper
2 cups diced cooked chicken
1 cup sliced celery
¼ cup sliced green onions
    Lettuce leaves
    Crumbled blue cheese (optional)

Combine mayonnaise, sour cream, lemon juice, sugar, lemon peel, mustard, salt and pepper in large bowl.

Add chicken, celery and green onions; stir to combine. Cover; refrigerate at least 1 hour to allow flavors to blend.

Serve salad on lettuce-lined plate. Sprinkle with blue cheese, if desired.

Makes 4 servings

NUTRIENTS PER SERVING: Carbohydrate: 4 g, Calories: 310, Fat: 23 g, Protein: 22 g

Spicy Oriental Shrimp Salad

   1 head iceberg lettuce
½ cup fresh basil leaves
¼ cup rice wine vinegar
   1 cube fresh ginger (2 inches), peeled
   1 tablespoon reduced-sodium soy sauce
   3 cloves garlic
   2 teaspoons dark sesame oil
   1 teaspoon red pepper flakes
 28 large raw shrimp, peeled and deveined
   1 to 2 limes, cut into wedges (optional)
      Vinaigrette Dressing (recipe follows)

Core, rinse and thoroughly drain lettuce. Refrigerate in airtight container to crisp. Combine basil, vinegar, ginger, soy sauce, garlic, sesame oil and red pepper in blender or food processor fitted with metal blade. Blend to form rough paste, pulsing blender on and off, scraping sides as needed. Transfer paste to large mixing bowl. Add shrimp and stir until coated. Cover; refrigerate for 2 hours or overnight.

Preheat broiler. Broil shrimp in shallow pan, turning once, just until pink, about 2 minutes on each side. Shred lettuce; arrange on four plates. Top with cooked shrimp. Garnish with lime, if desired. Serve with Vinaigrette Dressing.   *Makes 4 servings*

Vinaigrette Dressing: Whisk 3 tablespoons red wine vinegar with 1½ tablespoons olive oil in small bowl until blended.

NUTRIENTS PER SERVING: Carbohydrate: 7 g, Calories: 144, Fat: 8 g, Protein: 10 g

Greens and Broccoli Salad with Peppy Vinaigrette

4 sun-dried tomato halves (not packed in oil)
3 cups torn washed red-tipped or plain leaf lettuce
1½ cups broccoli flowerets
1 cup sliced fresh mushrooms
⅓ cup sliced radishes
2 tablespoons water
1 tablespoon balsamic vinegar
1 teaspoon vegetable oil
¼ teaspoon chicken bouillon granules
¼ teaspoon dried chervil, crushed
¼ teaspoon dry mustard
⅛ teaspoon ground red pepper

Pour enough boiling water over tomatoes in small bowl to cover. Let stand 5 minutes; drain. Chop tomatoes. Combine tomatoes, lettuce, broccoli, mushrooms and radishes in large salad bowl.

Combine 2 tablespoons water, vinegar, oil, bouillon granules, chervil, mustard and ground red pepper in jar with tight-fitting lid. Cover; shake well. Add to salad; toss to combine.

Makes 4 servings

NUTRIENTS PER SERVING: Carbohydrate: 9 g, Calories: 54, Fat: 2 g, Protein: 3 g

Greens and Broccoli Salad with Peppy Vinaigrette

Savory Sides

Grilled Vegetables

¼ cup minced fresh herbs, such as parsley, thyme, rosemary, oregano or basil
1 small eggplant (about ¾ pound), cut into ¼-inch-thick slices
½ teaspoon salt
1 *each* red, green and yellow bell pepper, quartered and seeded
2 zucchini, cut lengthwise into ¼-inch-thick slices
1 fennel bulb, cut lengthwise into ¼-inch-thick slices
   Nonstick cooking spray

1. Combine herbs in small bowl; let stand 3 hours or overnight.

2. Place eggplant in large colander over bowl; sprinkle with salt. Drain 1 hour.

3. Heat grill until coals are glowing red. Spray vegetables with cooking spray and sprinkle with herb mixture. Grill 10 to 15 minutes or until fork-tender and lightly browned on both sides. (Cooking times vary depending on type of vegetable; remove vegetables as they are done, to avoid overcooking.)   *Makes 6 servings*

Variation: Cut vegetables into 1-inch cubes and thread onto skewers. Spray with cooking spray and sprinkle with herb mixture. Grill as directed above.

NUTRIENTS PER SERVING: Carbohydrate: 8 g, Calories: 34, Fat: <1 g, Protein: 1 g

Marinated Mushrooms, Carrots and Snow Peas

1 cup julienne carrots
1 cup fresh snow peas or sugar snap peas
½ cup water
1 lemon
2 cups small mushrooms
⅔ cup white wine vinegar
2 tablespoons sugar
2 tablespoons extra-light olive oil
1 clove garlic, minced
2 tablespoons chopped fresh parsley
1 tablespoon chopped fresh thyme

1. Combine carrots and peas in 1-quart microwavable dish; add ½ cup water. Cover and microwave at HIGH 4 minutes or just until water boils. Do not drain.

2. Remove several strips of peel from lemon with vegetable peeler. Chop peel to measure 1 teaspoon. Squeeze juice from lemon to measure 2 tablespoons. Combine peel, juice and remaining ingredients in small bowl. Pour over carrot mixture. Cover and refrigerate at least 3 hours.

3. To serve, remove vegetables from marinade with slotted spoon. Place in serving dish; discard marinade.   *Makes 12 servings*

NUTRIENTS PER SERVING: Carbohydrate: 4 g, Calories: 30, Fat: 1 g, Protein: 1 g

Marinated Mushrooms, Carrots and Snow Peas

Broiled Zucchini Halves

Prep and Cook Time: 15 minutes

½ **cup (2 ounces) shredded mozzarella cheese**
2 **tablespoons diced pimiento**
2 **tablespoons chopped ripe olives**
4 **small zucchini (about 1 pound total), sliced lengthwise**
1 **tablespoon olive oil**

1. Preheat broiler; place oven rack 6 inches below heat source. Combine cheese, pimiento and olives in small bowl; set aside.

2. Brush both sides of zucchini halves with oil; arrange on broiler pan lined with foil. Broil 5 minutes or until fork-tender.

3. Spoon about 2 tablespoons cheese mixture along each zucchini half. Broil until cheese melts and browns. Serve immediately.   *Makes 4 side-dish servings*

NUTRIENTS PER SERVING: Carbohydrate: 4 g, Calories: 95, Fat: 7 g, Protein: 4 g

Broiled Zucchini Halves

Roasted Fall Vegetables

2 cups small broccoli florets
1 large red bell pepper, cut into squares
1 cup cubed turnip (1-inch cubes)
½ cup diced onion
2 teaspoons olive oil
1 tablespoon balsamic vinegar or red wine vinegar
½ cup fat-free reduced-sodium chicken broth or water
4 sprigs fresh thyme *or* ¼ teaspoon dried thyme leaves
¼ teaspoon salt
   Black pepper

1. Preheat oven to 425°F. Combine broccoli, bell pepper, turnip and onion in shallow heavy roasting pan.

2. Whisk together oil and vinegar; pour over vegetables, tossing to coat. Pour chicken broth around vegetables. Add thyme sprigs.

3. Roast vegetables about 30 minutes or until tender, stirring occasionally. Remove from oven. Season with salt and pepper.   *Makes 6 (⅓-cup) servings*

NUTRIENTS PER SERVING: Carbohydrate: 4 g, Calories: 36, Fat: 2 g, Protein: 2 g

Ratatouille

½ **pound eggplant, cut into ½-inch cubes**
1 **small onion, sliced and separated into rings**
1 **small zucchini, thinly sliced**
½ **medium green bell pepper, chopped**
1 **tomato, cut into wedges**
1 **tablespoon grated Parmesan cheese**
1 **rib celery, chopped**
¼ **teaspoon salt (optional)**
¼ **teaspoon dried chervil leaves**
¼ **teaspoon dried oregano leaves**
⅛ **teaspoon instant minced garlic**
⅛ **teaspoon dried thyme leaves**
   Dash ground pepper

Microwave Directions
Combine all ingredients in 2-quart microwavable casserole; cover. Microwave at HIGH
7 to 10 minutes or until eggplant is translucent, stirring every 3 minutes.

Makes 6 servings

NUTRIENTS PER SERVING: Carbohydrate: 6 g, Calories: 29, Fat: 1 g, Protein: 1 g

Ratatouille

Hot and Spicy Cabbage Medley

1 teaspoon CRISCO® Oil*
2 ounces smoked ham, chopped
½ cup chopped green bell pepper
½ cup chopped onion
1 can (10 ounces) tomatoes with green chilies, undrained and chopped
½ teaspoon sugar
4 cups sliced cabbage
⅛ teaspoon black pepper
⅛ teaspoon hot pepper sauce

Use your favorite Crisco Oil product.

1. Heat oil in large skillet on medium heat. Add ham, green pepper and onion. Cook and stir until vegetables are crisp-tender. Add tomatoes and sugar. Simmer 3 minutes.

2. Add cabbage, black pepper and hot pepper sauce. Simmer 15 minutes, stirring occasionally.   *Makes 8 servings*

NUTRIENTS PER SERVING: Carbohydrate: 5 g, Calories: 35, Fat: 1 g, Protein: 2 g

Sesame Broccoli

Prep Time: 1 minute   *Cook Time:* 8 to 9 minutes

1 bag (16 ounces) BIRDS EYE® frozen Broccoli Cuts
1 tablespoon sesame seeds
1 tablespoon oil
   Dash soy sauce (optional)

• Cook broccoli according to package directions.

• Cook sesame seeds in oil 1 to 2 minutes or until golden brown, stirring frequently.

• Toss broccoli with sesame seed mixture. Add soy sauce, salt and pepper to taste.

Makes 4 to 6 servings

NUTRIENTS PER SERVING: Carbohydrate: 6 g, Calories: 73, Fat: 5 g, Protein: 4 g

Zucchini with Pimiento

2 cups thinly sliced zucchini
1 small onion, chopped
1 jar (2 ounces) pimiento, drained and diced
½ teaspoon salt (optional)
½ teaspoon dried oregano leaves, crushed
⅛ teaspoon garlic powder
⅛ teaspoon ground red pepper

Microwave Directions
In 2-quart microwavable casserole, combine all ingredients; cover. Microwave at HIGH (100% power) 6 to 7 minutes or until fork-tender, stirring after half the cooking time.

Makes 4 servings

NUTRIENTS PER SERVING: Carbohydrate: 5 g, Calories: 22, Fat: <1 g, Protein: 1 g

Portobello Mushrooms Sesame

4 large portobello mushrooms
2 tablespoons sweet rice wine
2 tablespoons reduced-sodium soy sauce
2 cloves garlic, minced
1 teaspoon dark sesame oil

1. Remove and discard stems from mushrooms; set caps aside. Combine remaining ingredients in small bowl.

2. Brush both sides of mushrooms with soy sauce mixture. Grill mushrooms top side up on covered grill over medium coals 3 to 4 minutes. Brush tops with soy sauce mixture and turn over; grill 2 minutes more or until mushrooms are lightly browned. Turn again and grill, basting frequently, 4 to 5 minutes or until tender when pressed with back of spatula. Remove mushrooms and cut diagonally into $\frac{1}{2}$-inch-thick slices.   *Makes 4 servings*

NUTRIENTS PER SERVING: Carbohydrate: 9 g, Calories: 67, Fat: 2 g, Protein: 4 g

Hot and Spicy Spinach

1 red bell pepper, cut into 1-inch pieces
1 clove garlic, minced
1 pound prewashed fresh spinach, rinsed and chopped
1 tablespoon prepared mustard
1 teaspoon lemon juice
¼ teaspoon red pepper flakes

1. Spray large skillet with nonstick cooking spray; heat over medium heat. Add red bell pepper and garlic; cook and stir 3 minutes.

2. Add spinach; cook and stir 3 minutes or just until spinach begins to wilt.

3. Stir in mustard, lemon juice and red pepper flakes. Serve immediately.

Makes 4 servings

Tip: To obtain the maximum nutritional value from spinach, cook it for the shortest possible time. The vitamins in spinach and other greens are soluble in water and fats and are therefore lost during long cooking.

NUTRIENTS PER SERVING: Carbohydrate: 6 g, Calories: 37, Fat: 1 g, Protein: 4 g

Frenched Beans with Celery

¾ **pound fresh green beans**
 2 **ribs celery**
¼ **cup water**
 2 **tablespoons butter, melted**
 2 **tablespoons toasted sunflower seeds***
   Celery leaves and carrot slices for garnish

*To toast sunflower seeds, heat ½ teaspoon oil in small skillet over medium heat. Add shelled sunflower seeds; cook and stir 3 minutes or until lightly browned, shaking pan constantly. Remove with slotted spoon to paper towels.

1. Place beans in colander; rinse well. To prepare beans, snap off stem end from each bean, pulling strings down to remove if present. (Young tender beans may have no strings.)

2. Slice beans lengthwise; set aside.

3. To prepare celery, trim stem end and leaves from ribs. Reserve leaves for garnish, if desired. Slice ribs thin on the diagonal.

4. Bring 1 inch of water in 2-quart saucepan to a boil over high heat. Add beans and celery. Cover; reduce heat to medium-low. Simmer 8 minutes or until beans are crisp-tender; drain.

5. Toss beans and celery with butter. Transfer to warm serving dish. Sprinkle with sunflower seeds. Garnish, if desired. Serve immediately.   *Makes 6 side-dish servings*

NUTRIENTS PER SERVING: Carbohydrate: 4 g, Calories: 70, Fat: 6 g, Protein: 2 g

Frenched Beans with Celery

Light Lemon Cauliflower

¼ **cup chopped fresh parsley, divided**
½ **teaspoon grated lemon peel**
 6 **cups (about 1½ pounds) cauliflower florets**
 1 **tablespoon reduced-fat margarine**
 3 **cloves garlic, minced**
 2 **tablespoons fresh lemon juice**
¼ **cup grated Parmesan cheese**

1. Place 1 tablespoon parsley, lemon peel and about 1 inch of water in large saucepan. Place cauliflower in steamer basket and place in saucepan. Bring water to a boil over medium heat. Cover and steam 14 to 16 minutes or until cauliflower is crisp-tender. Remove to large bowl; keep warm. Reserve ½ cup hot liquid.

2. Heat margarine in small saucepan over medium heat. Add garlic; cook and stir 2 to 3 minutes or until soft. Stir in lemon juice and reserved liquid.

3. Spoon lemon sauce over cauliflower. Sprinkle with remaining 3 tablespoons parsley and cheese before serving. Garnish with lemon slices, if desired.   *Makes 6 servings*

NUTRIENTS PER SERVING: Carbohydrate: 6 g, Calories: 53, Fat: 2 g, Protein: 4 g

Light Lemon Cauliflower

Guiltless Zucchini

    Nonstick cooking spray
 4 medium zucchini, sliced
 $1/3$ cup chopped onion
 4 cloves garlic, minced
 $1/4$ teaspoon dried oregano leaves
 $1/2$ cup GUILTLESS GOURMET® Roasted Red Pepper Salsa
 $1/4$ cup (1 ounce) shredded low-fat mozzarella cheese

Coat large nonstick skillet with cooking spray; heat over medium heat until hot. Add zucchini; cook and stir 5 minutes. Add onion, garlic and oregano; cook 5 minutes more or until zucchini and onion are lightly browned. Stir in salsa. Bring just to a boil. Reduce heat to low; simmer 5 minutes more or until zucchini is crisp-tender. Sprinkle cheese on top; cover and cook 1 to 2 minutes or until cheese melts. Serve hot.   *Makes 4 servings*

NUTRIENTS PER SERVING: Carbohydrate: 8 g, Calories: 58, Fat: 1 g, Protein: 4 g

Italian Broccoli with Tomatoes

 4 cups broccoli florets
½ cup water
½ teaspoon dried Italian seasoning
½ teaspoon dried parsley flakes
¼ teaspoon salt (optional)
⅛ teaspoon black pepper
 2 medium tomatoes, cut into wedges
½ cup shredded part-skim mozzarella cheese

Microwave Directions

Place broccoli and water in 2-quart microwavable casserole; cover. Microwave at HIGH (100% power) 5 to 8 minutes or until crisp-tender. Drain. Stir in Italian seasoning, parsley, salt, pepper and tomatoes. Microwave, uncovered, at HIGH (100% power) 2 to 4 minutes or until tomatoes are hot. Sprinkle with cheese. Microwave 1 minute or until cheese melts.

Makes 6 servings

NUTRIENTS PER SERVING: Carbohydrate: 5 g, Calories: 50, Fat: 2 g, Protein: 4 g

Italian Broccoli with Tomatoes

The publisher would like to thank the companies and organizations listed below for the use of their recipes and photographs in this publication.

Birds Eye®

Del Monte Corporation

Delmarva Poultry Industry, Inc.

Florida Department of Citrus

Guiltless Gourmet®

The Kingsford Products Company

The Procter & Gamble Company

The Sugar Association, Inc.

Sunkist Growers

Tyson Foods, Inc.

Unilever Bestfoods North America

VOLUME MEASUREMENTS (dry)

$\frac{1}{8}$ teaspoon = 0.5 mL
$\frac{1}{4}$ teaspoon = 1 mL
$\frac{1}{2}$ teaspoon = 2 mL
$\frac{3}{4}$ teaspoon = 4 mL
1 teaspoon = 5 mL
1 tablespoon = 15 mL
2 tablespoons = 30 mL
$\frac{1}{4}$ cup = 60 mL
$\frac{1}{3}$ cup = 75 mL
$\frac{1}{2}$ cup = 125 mL
$\frac{2}{3}$ cup = 150 mL
$\frac{3}{4}$ cup = 175 mL
1 cup = 250 mL
2 cups = 1 pint = 500 mL
3 cups = 750 mL
4 cups = 1 quart = 1 L

VOLUME MEASUREMENTS (fluid)

1 fluid ounce (2 tablespoons) = 30 mL
4 fluid ounces ($\frac{1}{2}$ cup) = 125 mL
8 fluid ounces (1 cup) = 250 mL
12 fluid ounces (1$\frac{1}{2}$ cups) = 375 mL
16 fluid ounces (2 cups) = 500 mL

WEIGHTS (mass)

$\frac{1}{2}$ ounce = 15 g
1 ounce = 30 g
3 ounces = 90 g
4 ounces = 120 g
8 ounces = 225 g
10 ounces = 285 g
12 ounces = 360 g
16 ounces = 1 pound = 450 g

DIMENSIONS

$\frac{1}{16}$ inch = 2 mm
$\frac{1}{8}$ inch = 3 mm
$\frac{1}{4}$ inch = 6 mm
$\frac{1}{2}$ inch = 1.5 cm
$\frac{3}{4}$ inch = 2 cm
1 inch = 2.5 cm

OVEN TEMPERATURES

250°F = 120°C
275°F = 140°C
300°F = 150°C
325°F = 160°C
350°F = 180°C
375°F = 190°C
400°F = 200°C
425°F = 220°C
450°F = 230°C

BAKING PAN SIZES

Utensil	Size in Inches/Quarts	Metric Volume	Size in Centimeters
Baking or Cake Pan (square or rectangular)	8×8×2	2 L	20×20×5
	9×9×2	2.5 L	23×23×5
	12×8×2	3 L	30×20×5
	13×9×2	3.5 L	33×23×5
Loaf Pan	8×4×3	1.5 L	20×10×7
	9×5×3	2 L	23×13×7
Round Layer Cake Pan	8×1½	1.2 L	20×4
	9×1½	1.5 L	23×4
Pie Plate	8×1¼	750 mL	20×3
	9×1¼	1 L	23×3
Baking Dish or Casserole	1 quart	1 L	—
	1½ quart	1.5 L	—
	2 quart	2 L	—